# RO.
# 2014

Issue 22

# Home

Review of Postgraduate English Studies

Published by the Students of the MA in Literature and Publishing

Published by
The ROPES Team 2014
MA in Literature and Publishing
English Department
National University of Ireland, Galway

© ROPES 2014
All Contributors Retain the Rights to Their Own Works

ISBN: 987-1-908358-20-2

ISSN: 0791-8054

Cover Design by Declan Devlin

Logo Design by Moira Morley

Printed in the Republic of Ireland
by Gemini International Ltd
Dublin

# Acknowledgements

ROPES 2014 would not have been possible without the assistance of a number of people. We thank Dr Julia Carlson Kilroy, Dearbhla Mooney, Rob Smyth, Toner Quinn and the English Department of the National University of Ireland, Galway for their continued guidance and support.

To all of our authors and artists, we thank you for your contributions and for keeping up the high standard of ROPES. We would also like to extend our thanks to Niamh Boyce for her contribution as a featured writer, to the Cúirt International Festival of Literature and COPE Galway for their support and inspiration.

Lastly, we would like to thank you, the reader. By purchasing this book you have given it meaning and helped the community of Galway in the process.

## Table of Contents

**Foreword** ................................................................... i

**A Brief Word for Rooms** .......................................... 1
Trevor Conway

**The Table** ................................................................. 5
Aoife McCollum

**Coming Home** ......................................................... 6
Margarita Gokun

**Home for the Night** ................................................. 7
Brian Hickey

**Henry St.** ................................................................. 10
Kate Ennals

**Our Attic** ................................................................. 12
Alvy Carragher

**Thunder and Ice Cream** .......................................... 14
Padhraic Harris

**Long Walk Home** .................................................... 17
Sarah Devaney

**Visitor** ..................................................................... 18
Breda Spaight

**Spindlewood** ........................................................... 19
Anne Marie Kennedy

The Memories That Thaw .................................... 22
Christopher Meehan

Teach Mhamó .................................................... 23
Fiona Nic Dhonnacha

Salthill Ferris Wheel ......................................... 25
Ruth Quinlan

A Map ............................................................. 28
Brian Kirk

Tapies ............................................................. 30
Jerry Wemple

Mourne Cottage ................................................ 32
Marion Clarke

The Pin and the Plait ........................................ 33
Paul Lewis

Simple Quietude ............................................... 37
Máire Morrissey-Cummins

Llewyn Davis, Bringing It All Back Home .......... 38
Tim Dwyer

Tom ............................................................... 39
Niamh Boyce

Murphy, Portmarnock Strand ............................ 40
Kate Quigley

Saint, Sea and the Cyclops of Tory Island ......... 41
Anne Irwin

*Home*

**Teeth** .................................................................... 42
Maureen Gallagher

**Darkness Is the Absence** ........................................ 43
Dean Buckley

**Our Downstairs Landlady's Request to My Mother, London NW 7, 1969** ............................................. 44
Kevin Higgins

**Octopus Still Growing, Fleeing Visitors Warn** ........ 46
Jessamine O Connor

**Octopus** ................................................................. 48
Rebecca Connell

**On the Hill there Is a Tree** .................................... 49
Máire T. Robinson

**Family Vault** .......................................................... 54
Aideen Henry

**There Are Two Ways** ............................................. 56
Brooke Randel

**Home for Christmas** .............................................. 58
Kate Quigley

**Armageddon and Rusheen Bay** .............................. 60
Anne Irwin

**Not** ........................................................................ 61
Kevin Higgins

**The Sugarloaf Mountain, Co. Wicklow, Ireland ... 62**
Máire Morrissey-Cummins

**To the Second Born .................................................. 63**
Ruth Quinlan

**What Sarah Knows .................................................. 64**
Alvy Carragher

**The Move .............................................................. 68**
Rachael Hanaphy-Pigott

**Kids in School ........................................................ 70**
Faye Boland

**They Sold Their Calves in Spring ............................ 71**
Helen Hughes

**Nomad .................................................................. 76**
Aideen Henry

**New Tricks for Me and Ma ..................................... 77**
Nerina Burke

**Étain Moves in with Fúamnach ............................... 78**
**Étain in Fúamnach's Thrall ..................................... 79**
**Étain in Fúamnach's Spell ....................................... 80**
Ann Egan

**La Belle Bitch ........................................................ 82**
Niamh Boyce

**Housey .................................................................. 83**
Nerina Burke

*Home*

**Sunroom, Midnight** ....................................................... 84
David J. Doyle

**Little Maverick Hen** ...................................................... 86
Faye Boland

**I Used to Sit by the Water and
Watch the Waves Rolling By** ........................................ 87
Vincent Hughes

**Dringeen Bay** ................................................................ 88
Vincent Hughes

**Seeking Light** ................................................................ 90
Máire Morrissey-Cummins

**Nature's Healing Hands** ............................................... 91
Máire Morrissey-Cummins

**Contributors** ................................................................. 94

**The ROPES Team** ....................................................... 104

## Foreword

For twenty-two years, the students of the National University of Ireland's MA in Literature and Publishing have been producing the ROPES literary journal. This year, the team decided to collaborate with and donate all proceeds to COPE Galway, a charity that has been providing social services to the Galway community for decades. In keeping with COPE's vision of "improved quality of life in a home of your own", the theme of this year's publication is "home". The following poems, short stories and artwork selections are depictions of what home can mean to different people from all sorts of "homes".

This year, as project manager, I have had the pleasure of working with the great publishing team that is the MA in Literature and Publishing class of 2014, a selection of talented writers and artists, and the endlessly helpful and supportive staff at NUI Galway. Without them, ROPES would not be the exceptional product it is today.

What follows in this journal represents not only depictions of home in its geographical or physical sense, but home as a person, place, time or abstract idea.

*Siobhán Keenan*
*Project Manager*

# A Brief Word for Rooms

*Hallway*

Welcome! Step inside.
Visitors, please clean your feet.
My carpet, there's talk of covering it
In wood, hard as a horse's shoe.
A brown tinge shows in the light,
But what of it?
I am the sea, connecting lands,
Bearing calls: "Dinner!"
I lift the stairs into the sky,
Listen to the various lilts of steps,
The swish of coats on the banister post,
The hushed phone calls that follow closed doors.
Light changes as I see you off to work
And greet you when the day is done.

*Dining Room*

Oh, I've seen it all:
The laden plates of a special occasion,
The wine and toasts, the photo-flash,
The burnt reminiscence and argument to follow.
I have seen pepper ground to mottled specks
Of green, black, red, and brown.
Candle flames waver as arms reach out,
So much geometry in coasters and plates,
Forks and knives, tables and chairs.
The only irregular shapes among it all
Move their bending arms
And bulging cheeks.

*Kitchen*

I'll aspire to be bright and sleek.
Fluorescent. Daylight. Whatever's quickest.

# Home

You'll hear me hum and sizzle, see me stain,
Drawers punched in with a rattle.
Steam. Fast. Fog. Windows:
Perhaps an act of affection.
Odours of coffee, fish, cheese, onion:
Perhaps necessity.
All conveniently compartmentalised,
I will be your watering hole,
Where you converse, your body
Constantly turning.
Sometimes, you'll linger,
But mostly you'll be going,
Moving on.

### Utility Room

I would speak in a whisper
If I spoke at all.
I'm small, quite undernourished.
If I had a human name,
You'd call me Frank,
Embarrassed by the occasional rumble
Lasting an hour,
Wincing as the dog gets in,
Waiting for the fuss of voices,
But I'd never take up
Much of your time.

### Sitting Room

I have warmed you by the fire,
Put a glass of swirling brandy in your hand,
Invited you to doze,
Speak, smoke, or recline
On the soft, bending surface of cushion.
And I have heard you laugh many times,
Or shout, mostly at the TV,
Beaming unmistakable green.

Occasional parties have spilled into me,
Easy chatter circling 'round
The dim burst of the corner lamp,
Curtains drawn at dark
To complete the colour scheme.
I have seen little girls on laps,
Kisses, arms thrown around necks.
I have been, all along,
Your friend, your child, your lover.

*Bathroom*

Are you happy with how you look?
I'll tell you how you look,
And won't care that you stare so much,
Though there's only so much to discover.
I am devoted to your body,
Determined to secure well-being.
Your visitors ask for me,
Perhaps smiling at funny signs,
Ruffling the mat over cold tile
Or reading folded paper.
I harbour rain, rivers, and lakes.
Please open the window as you leave.

*Bedroom*

There will be time for thought,
Licking the walls with solitude, space,
For staring past the window as you perceive
Life as it is, as it could be,
Objects lining the windowsill,
Scented candles, a dust-stranded desk.
The bed will be your centrepiece,
A thick cocoon to make you new.
Open the curtains, the wardrobe door,
And choose what will follow.
I will be your first and last,

*Home*

The one to bid you
Good morning and good night.

*Trevor Conway*
*Dunally, Co. Sligo*

# The Table

We all sit at the table of a house we loved,
where we laughed
and ate homemade chips –
Blind Date on the television –
Saturday evening bliss.

Rummaging in hedges,
making bird cages,
forming secret passageways –
the days of infinite youthfulness.

Dancing,
joking,
falling out,
and forgetting why –
ungratefully happy below the blue sky.

Old before our day,
we sit at the same table, in the same house –
facing the grieving morning –
with only echoes and silhouettes
to comfort our
broken hearts.

*Aoife McCollum*
*Letterkenny and Galway*

*Home*

# Coming Home

*Margarita Gokun*
*Madrid, Spain*

## Home for the Night

He pushes his hand deeper and retrieves a part-eaten burger from beneath the pile of food scraps and other rubbish that fills the bin to the top. The meat smells a bit rank, but it's been a long night and the steady, painful gurgling in his gut encourages him to finish what someone else started. There's a sharp wind blowing along the canal and he huddles behind the wall while he finishes breakfast. A blind twitches open in the spruced-up tenement block opposite, where a smartly dressed girl looks down on him. She is joined by an older man, who points down at him and mimics a phone being held to his ear. He takes the hint, puts the duffel bag onto his shoulder, and starts walking along the canal towards the city centre.

It's only a mile, but the sole of his right shoe is worn through and the edges rub hard against cracked skin on his ankle, so it's an hour before he reaches the centre. He pulls out a dirty old blanket, a battered coffee cup, and a rough written sign announcing his plight and sits down. It's Tuesday, so he has low expectations on a return for his effort, but it's a sheltered spot and he gets a waft of warm air when the door to the pub beside him opens. He used to play a tin whistle in the vain hope that passers-by would reward his effort, if not talent, but that went months ago, a fair swap for a couple of fags and an owed favour. Now he relies on a gentle smile and his dark eyes that still shine, occasionally attracting a sympathetic smile and a few coins in return.

Manky Malky shuffles up, pulled semi-erect by his one-eyed dog, and shouts while swaying and holding out a nearly empty bottle of cheap sherry.

"Awright son, have a swallie."

He shakes his head and mutters a no with a half-smile.

"Suit yerself. Just watch oot fur they bastarts by the way."

He follows Malky's unsteady finger to the group on the other side of the road and recognises the Albanians he had the run-in with a few days ago. The five of them are smoking and one is eating an onion. The rip in his jacket, and the crisp, black blood surrounding it, reminds him he needs to be careful when they're around.

The pub kitchen staff begins to cook dinner, and he can hear the clatter of plates and banter from the kitchen staff as they busy themselves. His gut rumbles in response to the thick, beefy aroma and he surveys the blanket for options, but it's been a slow day and there's only an inch of copper coins in the cup, and a handful more on the blanket. He'll have to cadge his tea and he needs to get sorted for tonight.

He shuffles along the road, to the side door of Pret, and catches the eye of the manager in the kitchen, who disappears back into the main shop and returns with a sandwich, a couple of battered pastries and a bottle of water.

"There ye go, pal."

An older woman glares at him from behind and shakes her head in disgust.

"That's against policy, Mike."

"Aye well, policies are fur politicians. The stuff's gaun in the bin anyway." He smiles and winks.

It's getting dark; the offices are emptying and the streets are filling up as he becomes invisible again, sheltering in the alley beside the shop and stuffing the food into his mouth. The wind has picked up and he feels the first stinging drops of cold rain on his face. Shivering to the bone, he pulls an ancient cagoule from the duffel and wraps it around himself. It's only half a mile to the overnight hostel but he'll need to get a move on as the beds will have gone by seven o'clock on a night like this. He walks down the long road towards the river, his slow gait and unkempt appearance a counterpoint to the workers hurrying home.

A dirty white van pulls up beside him and he recognises the girl as she leans over the passenger seat and winds down the window.

"Hiya. Ye gaun tae the centre? Better hurry up, they storms huv done in the roof and wuv loast the whole tap flair and wur doon aboout ten beds."

The girl sees the disappointment in his face and smiles back in encouragement. He tries to push on a bit harder, biting his lip as the shoes dig deeper and the wound in his side stabs harder, but the wind is strong across the exposed bridge. He can only manage a shuffle until he gets to the other side and finds respite behind a wall of billboards waving their messages at the speeding traffic.

Reaching the centre, he sees there's a queue that is steadily dwindling as the ragged group is counted through the gate by one of the centre staff. He looks for the English guy, Joel, but there's no sign of him. As he gets closer to the front of the queue, he sees the Albanians come out of a shop and make a run towards the centre. The youngest grabs his jacket just as he is getting to the gate, says something unintelligible, and smacks him hard in the face and onto the ground. Nonplussed, the centre worker waves the five Albanians through just as a girl sticks her head out the door.

"That's us full, tell them there might be space at Rutherglen."

He groans as that's miles away and much smaller, so there's no chance he'll get a bed. He can't cope with another night outside. Through the gate, the young Albanian gives him a violent stare, reminding him they have unfinished business. The few others who didn't get in start to walk away in pursuit of other options and he's left sitting on the pavement feeling crushed and tasting blood.

Joel appears, helps him up and pushes him through the gate and into the centre.

"What a mess. I've told you before to stay away from them. Here, it's your lucky night." He opens the door to a room with a single bed.

"No rush tomorrow, you can help me do some cleaning and grab some lunch before you head off. I'll fix you up with some warmer clothes as well."

The room is sparse but clean, with a shower room that has basic toiletries, including a much-needed razor. There's a gentle hiss from the radiator and the cityscape through the window is blurred by condensation. He unzips the duffel and takes out a poly bag that has the clean t-shirt and underwear he's been saving. He peels off his filthy clothes and piles them in the corner from where the fetid smell of dried sweat starts to fill the room.

Standing under the stream of sharply hot water, he lathers soap and rubs it over his bony frame, wincing as he washes the dried blood off the scar in his side, and watches the water gradually run clean. It takes him fifteen minutes of gentle hacking with the cheap razor before he's able to run his hand over smooth skin. There's nothing he can do about his hair though; he'll add that to the list of favours he'll ask of Joel tomorrow.

He takes the cardboard box out of the duffel, unfurls the bubble wrap that is holding it together, and pulls out the picture. Carolyn and the girls smile brightly at him, a sea of blonde and blue, and he places it on the table beside the bed. Lying back, unable to keep his eyes open, he drifts off. He'd forgotten what home was like.

*Brian Hickey*
*Glasgow, Scotland*

*Home*

## Henry St.

I fill you with geraniums and jasmine,
candles, and yellow primroses from the garden.
I flavour you with chillies, garlic, dusty potatoes, ginger, brown bread, salmon
with a squeeze of lemon.

I line you with books,
draft you with words, paper them across walls.
They spill over, hang in corners
spinning cautionary tales.

I lie in my iron bed of white sheets,
watch children hold hands as they go to school.
Late at night, when age has taken its toll
I hear their older, drunken screams drool

From their twisted lips.

Awake, I make cups of tea: green, Earl Grey, rooibos.
It could be three AM or four PM.
I listen to the BBC World Service.
I wash up one plate, one knife, one fork, one glass, one pot.

Home in Henry St.

*Kate Ennals*
*Of the World*

## Postgraduate Programme

**MA in Literature & Publishing**
A programme that merges scholarship in literature with studies in the elements of publishing. Courses include textual studies of various periods, editing, publishing law, marketing and business studies as well as theoretical reflections on present publishing practices.

*Contact Dr Julia Carlson Kilroy,*
T: +353 91 493786
E: julia.kilroy@nuigalway.ie

**Entry Requirements, Number of Places, Duration, and Deadline:**
Applicants must hold a B.A. degree or equivalent, with a minimum standard of Honours 2.2 overall and Honours 2.1 in one subject or equivalent (USA: BA at GPA 3.00). The programme is limited to 15-20 students, and extends full-time for one year (September-August).

**Applications should be made online at http://www.pac.ie**

Please contact the Admissions Office at postgradadmissions@nuigalway.ie or see **http://www.nuigalway.ie/courses/taught-postgraduate-courses/literature-publishing.html**

**English Department Website address: http://www.nuigalway.ie/enl/**

*Home*

## Our Attic

Lemon low-slung walls
softly leaned into us,
half of Bambi
made his way across the lower wall.
There was almost enough time
to finish the murals,
the wooden floors
splattered in the colours of our dreams,
glitter and grit trapped between boards.

The small square of a window
too high for us then;
we'd pull the stool under it
scrabble up, curl into it to watch
the seasons go by
or perhaps to spy on Daddy's working men.

That same window,
where once my sister left her pet frog in
a lunch box, only to find it fried flat later.

There was a clown that hung for a while,
in the centre of our childhood kingdom
on a swing, with a porcelain face so jeer –
smooth. When I was old enough to reach,
he disappeared, a paid vacation; let's
not ask questions we don't want the answers to.
Glass dolls in the back of the
room that I wanted to crack the faces off.

There was a solid line down the middle;
I would brush the mess to my sister's side
where it belonged, and keep the chaos from
spilling onto me. Occasionally we would
switch sides, spend a day heaving things
across the room and reinvent ourselves

on the other side, to inevitably move back again
when rain kept us from other places.

There was a spiral staircase:
a lethal thing, the stuff of fairytales and
we would wheel down that banister like
lunatics, until my brother took a tumble
and for a week we stepped with care.

At night we'd grip the top step and hang our
heads upside down to peep downstairs
at explicit TV shows, the horrors of Hannibal
Lecter at eight years old.
We spent the night
not in but under our beds, whispering
Hail Marys, and wondered for weeks about
our parents and the things they watched.

Sometimes we played foxes and rabbits,
constructed tunnels across the room,
of bent up mattresses and upturned
tables. We'd nibble kitchen carrots,
a special treat, and just that once the fox could
have one too.

In time, Bambi got blotted out
and floors refinished, to sell it all off,
but you can't get glitter out of years of grit,
no matter how fresh or thick the coat of paint.

*Alvy Carragher*
*Wherever My Family Is*

## Thunder and Ice Cream

Huddled under the stairs we counted out the time with a short pause after each number... one, (pause) two, (pause)... this time as far as eight.
And then the clap, the roll, the noise, the thunder.
"Mammy, is it far away?" I asked.
"A long way away, miles and miles away," she said.
I sighed. I was afraid of the thunder and lightning but Mammy told me I was the man of the house today. I was seven and I had to be brave. My sister, Rita, who was only four and fast asleep, needed me to be strong for both of them.
Just last year a man from down the road was hit by lightning and died. He was filling a bucket from the river. We did not want that to happen to us. Mammy said that would be a terrible way to go. And so unlucky. Like the chance of your number coming up in the sweepstake, but in a bad way.
The stairs were just inside the front door. Underneath was open with plenty of room for us all. There was only the one room downstairs. The other room was a shop.
There was a big front window where the table was. Granddad liked to sit there when he came to stay for his holidays. He had a great view of all the comings and goings to the shop. At the back of the room was another big window and a sink in front of it. In between was the range with a chimney.
As Mammy said, the house was the world's worst during a thunderstorm. It was all windows, doors, taps and a chimney. The world's worst.
Flash! We counted: one, two, three, four, five, six.
"Is it going to come here?" I asked.
"It's a little bit closer but still a long, long way away from here."
"Down near the river?"
"Oh, even further than that. We'll be safe here no matter what. Isn't it cosy? Rita's the lucky one to be fast asleep, all cuddled up in Daddy's coat, with her brother looking after her. Snug as a bug in a rug."
The door to the shop was just beside us. The bell hadn't rung since the thunder and lightning started. Everybody was probably at home huddled under their own stairs, counting out loud like we were.
It had started to rain. We could hear it hitting against the window and the glass of the door. "Lashing rain," was what my mother said it was doing. "That will help to cool the air down. It will be over soon."
It was dark now. "Pitch dark," my mother said. The lights had gone

out. Lucky she had plugged out our new television because lightning could come down the aerial too. I would never think of things like that if I was in charge by myself.

She said that under the stairs was the safest place in the house. The lightning would have to be very smart to find us and anyway it would have to bend and dive and everyone knows lightning doesn't do that.

Just then the shop bell rang.

"Who in the name of God could that be, out in the middle of all this. Well whoever it is they can wait. I'm not going out there," Mammy said.

Then another flash. One, two, three, four. Only four now. Boom boom. Like giant rocks rolling down a valley. That is what I said and she said that was very good, it was exactly what it sounded like.

"I'm afraid," I said.

"We'll be alright. The rain will cool it down. It's a long way from here."

"Mammy, don't leave me in charge if you go out to the shop."

"I'm not going out there, whoever it is can wait."

And then came the brightest flash of them all and Mammy let out a gasp and I grabbed her. It was like it was in the house itself. I was frightened. I was the man of the house but I was no good at it and I began to cry. Whoever was in the shop banged a coin on the counter for someone to come out.

"Is there anyone in there?" a woman shouted.

"Who could it possibly be?" said my mother, "I'd better go out and get rid of her. Stay where you are and you will be all right."

"No, Mammy, don't leave us."

"I'll leave the door open so I can hear you," and she went out to the shop.

Rita was still asleep but moved her foot a bit. I could hear voices from the shop and then Mammy shouting, the bell ringing and the door shutting. Mammy came back in and put her arm around me. "That Nora Hanratty needs her head examined," she said.

"Why does Nora Hanratty need her head examined?" I asked.

"Oh God, don't ever call her Nora, she's Mrs Hanratty to you," she said, "and 'having her head examined' is just a figure of speech. She was looking for a batch loaf and candles. I told her she was mad to be out in this weather but she said it was nothing compared to New York, where she spent years. There were no loaves left but plenty of sliced pans. She said she wouldn't have anything to do with a sliced pan, but then squeezed them all and said they were all stale anyway. She took the candles and said it was no way to talk to a customer, calling her 'mad', and she would never darken our door again. I told her it was just that it was dangerous to be out in the thunderstorm, but there was no talking to her. Mark my words: she'll be back again when it suits her or when Grogans' is closed on the Sunday."

While she was talking about Mrs Hanratty, we hardly noticed that the thunder and lightning had died down and the place was brightening up again.

"Well I suppose Mrs Hanratty did some good; at least she took our minds off the thunder," Mammy said.

The lights were still off.

"Will the ice cream in the fridge start to melt," I asked, "like it did the last time?"

"Not for a good while yet. Thank God the fridge is fairly empty anyway so there won't be much lost."

"Do you remember the last time when you said I was a great help eating some of the ice cream, and you cut two big sixpenny ice creams before it melted? Will we have to do that again?"

"Depends on how long the ESB is gone, but, just to be on the safe side, I think there are two choc ices out there on the top that could be starting to melt. It would be as well to eat them, I suppose, so they don't spoil the rest. What do you think?"

*Padhraic Harris*
*Galway*

# Long Walk Home

*Sarah Devaney*
*Castlebar*

*Home*

## Visitor

Hardly anyone calls
to our house anymore.
The rooms are dying;
their blood bleeds
in dusty corners, cobweb
hammocks strung from picture
frames between windows.
The ones who do visit –
the returned cousins from
England, America – blow the
horn of the rented car at the gate.
They wait for you to open
the door, but word has gone out,
as word does when hedges
become unkempt, dahlias turn brown
on rotten stems, skeleton figures
in December.
The car moves off.
The lace curtain shifts with your breath.

*Breda Spaight*
*Limerick*

## Spindlewood

I was their unnatural child, transplanted without roots and they grew me there, in three rooms under thatch, with a flat roof at the back where they trapped the rainwater for washing. They had tea chests full of turf and geranium covered pots in a porch, behind a varnished half-door.

Families of cats slept under lace curtains on wide windowsills, or under the range in baskets she lined with remnants from stitching. A suck lamb was bottle fed in the scullery where wellingtons got left on faded check lino. The black kettle sang, the cuckoo clock rang and the flowery tea caddy rattled when she put it back on the plank that they called a mantel.

Climbing roses got twisted around pillars and trellised up gables – bastards for pruning, he said, but the thorns were for clinging to pebble-dash or up the timber arch she said. How else would they reach up and climb if they didn't have fingers and his hands would be torn when he'd prune the nude stems in springtime.

My iron bed was piled high with heavy blankets, handmade pillows, a hot water jar under a feather eiderdown and the whiff of paraffin oil that was like lavender at bedtime.

She made supper from nothing – a slice of toast and a kipper, a hard-boiled egg and cheese or a slice of tart I had a hand in. They talked of the fairies and ghosts to frighten or delight me and by the light of the tilley lamp, their stories enlightened me.

The *meitheal* came with the thresher and perched themselves on seats around the small kitchen table – strong men and lads with vests on, loud voices, thirsty from tossing and pitching. Throats, dry from the chaff, were wetted with pots of strong tea or sometimes black porter. They made tall cocks of straw and tied them down in the haggard. They bagged the oats from the chute and I shouted at rats from a safe distance, on a stile by the gate in the orchard.

When I was eight, a boy came and I asked him to marry me there, on the third rung, while our brown legs hung down and we sucked blackcurrants from a canister.

After she died, a cold-hearted woman told me I was her natural niece. I lied with confidence, said I knew all along because they had grafted me securely onto their branches.

I thrived in their light and I now live in that house I was cherished in. I have climbers that wind around pillars and up gable walls and my fingers

*Home*

bleed in the springtime, but her roses are worth it.

*Anne Marie Kennedy*
*Craughwell, Co. Galway*

## The Lane Studio

Graduation Photography
&
Parchment Framing service Galway.

www.thelanestudios.com
091-567938

## BIG-O-TAXIS
### 091 CALL
### 58•58•58

Big O Taxis - Serving the students of Galway for over 30 years. We operate a complete taxi service 24/7, 365 days a year, to the domestic and commercial sector.

We are continually striving to bring value to the students of Galway, and we fully recognise the continued financial pressure put on students today given the current economic climate, that is why we have introduced set fares, discount cards and we will continue to review these.

The Mission of Big O Taxis is to attract and retain customers by providing a first Class Taxi Service and fostering a disciplined culture of safety, service, and trust.

# CHARLIE BYRNE'S
## BOOKSHOP ~ SIOPA LEABHAR
### WINNER OF THE BEST BOOKSHOP IN IRELAND 2013

New Books • Bargain Books • Secondhand Books
Ordering • Gift Vouchers • Book Shipping

THE CORNSTORE, MIDDLE ST., GALWAY

Ph. (091) 561766 - www.charliebyrne.com
Facebook.com/CharlieByrnesBookshop
Twitter: @ByrnesBooks

CELEBRATING 25 YEARS IN BUSINESS

## The Memories That Thaw

Lost in a new life, I take in the old place
Where six was a lot to get in, and pillows
Told of children who slept with too much sand
In their hair. So strange to stand on the wrong
Side of those windows, conjuring up the faces
Forever looking outward at the sea that
Always promised to lullaby the night.

These are the memories that thaw in spite
Of cold storage, that seep from the mind flooding
The heart but too fast, just like the sea that once
Broke its promise and turned the backroom into
The edge of the Atlantic as we huddled
In the darkness during the storms of '91.

*Christopher Meehan*
*Kilkee, Co. Clare*

## Teach Mhamó

A little white bungalow
Where I spent most of my childhood
In content companionship with my Mamó.
We ate her *cáca baile* and sipped tea
at the scuffed kitchen table
that propped many elbows through many years of conversation, laughter, tears.
We spent afternoons on the couch
Watching Dallas on the clunky television in the corner
She gave me 7UP when I was sick,
Which I sipped, pitifully, while she kept watch beside me and knitted
with deft fingers, needles clicking softly in rhythm with the grandfather clock's ticking,
I dozed in the comfort of my surroundings.

She lit a candle on New Year's Eve
In reverence to the Holy Face
framed in every room, His arms held out in solemn embrace.
But that night we witnessed His betrayal:
He smote His flames upon the house,
Blazing through every room, relentless.
The fire brigade was too late.
We could only watch, helpless,
as fire greedily devoured
the soul
of a house that shaped lives and held countless memories
Until only the blackened shell was left.
Empty. Cold.

Now Mamó sits quietly, her delicate hands clasped
on the blanket spread across her lap,
Surrounded by yellow walls and pallid faces,
She looks at us, bewildered,
Lost among people she doesn't know

## Home

And asks when can she
Go home.

*Fiona Nic Dhonnacha*
*An Cheathrú Rua, Co. na Gaillimhe*

## Salthill Ferris Wheel

I'm eager for a bird's perspective
on a place I know at sea level.
For the chance to see Galway Bay
through the pinhole stare of a seagull.
I've passed the fairground many times
during penance on the Prom –
dismissing it as the tourists' gaudy bauble.
But this week, life is flat. Ironed out.
The routine's carving furrows in my head.

I slide into the cherry-red seat,
ignoring raindrops on the plastic as
the attendant swings and snaps
a steel bar across my lap.
His rough efficiency makes it easy
to surrender safety to a stranger –
to a man who flashes sand-boy grins
as the great wheel shudders
and I am raised above him.

The air is heavy
with burned caramels of candyfloss,
the buttered saltiness of popcorn –
the fragrance of summer holidays
and sublimated teenage desire.

The couple below begin to kiss,
dark hair falling across a cloud
of white, whipped sugar
until her fingers uncurl and open
as she reaches to cup his cheek.
The forgotten floss swirls and tumbles,
landing in the carnival dust.

*Home*

I comfort myself with toffee
and watch the sea watching me.

*Ruth Quinlan*
*Tralee, Co. Kerry*

## Medieval Studies
### NUI, Galway

### Post-Graduate Medieval Studies: MA & PhD

NUI Galway offers **2 postgraduate degree options in Medieval Studies:**
- a **1-yr (12 month) taught MA,** with minor dissertation of 15,000 words;
- a **4-yr Structured PhD,** with thesis of 80,000 words (*unique in Ireland*).

Students are encouraged to view the Irish & European past in a multidimensional way while acquiring a thorough grounding in the study of languages, cultures and society from Late Antiquity to the end of the Middle Ages.

Gaining the skills necessary for innovative academic research, students take a combination of core modules (including palaeography & Latin) and electives in archaeology, history, literature and medieval vernacular languages (including Old Irish, Anglo-Saxon, Middle High German, Old French, Icelandic).
*No prior knowledge of Latin or these languages is required.*

Both programmes foster teamwork and contribute to graduates' wider expertise that can lead either to PhD research and university appointments or employment in several arenas outside of academia. Students
- complete an Internet-based *scriptorium* project;
- contribute to *IMBAS*, an international postgraduate medievalists' conference;
- PhD students complete a *project-based module* & gain practical experience either within the university or in the wider community

**Entry Requirements:**
Applicants must hold a B.A. degree or equivalent (NFQ level 8), at a minimum standard of Honours 2nd Class, Grade 1 (USA: B.A. at GPA 3.3).

MAs consist of 2 semesters of course work & a dissertation completed in the summer. PhDs complete course work and thesis research & writing in 4 years.

Application should be made on line at http://www.pac.ie/

**Contact:**
**Dr Kimberly LoPrete**
T +353 91 493 547
E *kim.loprete@nuigalway.ie*

**Further information available at:**
http://www.nuigalway.ie/medievalstudies/

## A Map

all he has is a map
        in his head
of a few crooked fields
        scarred by train tracks
        hemmed in by salt water
and a burgeoning town

sometimes he goes back there
        to pick at the past
to leave the imprint of
        his shoe in old mud
        the sea wind on his face
with his back to the town

he walks the few miles
        in his dreams
'til he comes to the house
        back to front now
        since the road moved
concealing its sacred junk

he opens the back door
        never the front
and steps into the past
        affected by pity and love
        for those who lived there
with him once now all gone

the map is a child's drawing
        scrawled crayon

on raw nerves etched in guilt
        carefully rolled by an adult
        a scroll from a story where
x denotes buried treasure

*Brian Kirk*
*Rush, Co. Dublin*

## Tapies

Hot summers we played ball in the carnival lot
using tapies: old baseballs, covers worn and gone,
held together by quarter rolls of electrical tape

pilfered out of our fathers' garages or bought
from the discount bin in Guffey's Hardware
with pennies and nickels earned from bottles

redeemed at Jean's corner store.
Those summers were hot, even hotter than these days.
Mornings we'd be out by eight, the air already

heavy, sky filled with a haze that would remain
until the evening rains. We'd pound the ball all
summer, using wooden bats too long or too short,

too heavy for our arms. With tapies, even the kids
without mitts could catch a fly ball, though we usually
had enough gloves to go around if we picked sides carefully

and shared. Those days our fathers, or worse,
our stepfathers, laid off from the mill would drink
cheap drafts from noontime on down at Shaffer's Tavern,

watching the Phillies lose again on an old-style set
with rabbit ears and adjustable dials, mounted
sturdily on a corner shelf next to the Schmidt's

beer clock. The men would grouse about the heat,
about the snow last winter, about maybe moving
to Florida, someplace where there was no need

for the expense of winter coats and winter tires.
And sometimes in the fall a kid would be missing:
Bobby, or Timmy Mathis who lived a few blocks over

past the Spruce Street cemetery and who none of us
much liked anyway. Still, he was good for another
outfielder, willing to play catcher, and now he was gone,

disappeared. Our fathers would sweat as they walked
the afternoon blocks home, just in time to cut the backyard
before supper. We'd scuttle home too, dusty, scraped,

our shirts and hair matted wet. After supper, our fathers
might take a call on the kitchen phone from a cousin
who says they're hiring drivers up at the bread plant.

But more than likely they'd go out on the back porch
with one more bottle of F&S beer and think about how
two years ago, when the mine shut down in the town

over the mountain, six hundred union jobs just disappeared.
And we'd drift back over to the carnie lot for a few more
innings, play a few minutes past when it was too dark

to see the ball. Fireflies would be blinking in the deep
outfield. And when it was our turn to bat, we'd swing
with all our might, smack that crinkled cover of the make-do ball,

hoping to make it safely home.

*Jerry Wemple*
*Pennsylvania, United States*

*Home*

## Mourne Cottage

*Marion Clarke*
*Warrenpoint*

## The Pin and the Plait

He has seen her and she has seen him. Two hundred yards still separate them. She hides behind her slanting fringe, one eye completely obscured, the other squeezes over like somebody trying to share a small umbrella. He attempts a nonchalant gait and fails absolutely. His legs are ready to revolt, take control of themselves, coil around one another and trip him up. He takes his hands from his pockets and puts them back in again. He takes out one and finally the other. They are close now, just a lady with shopping between them. Their eyes meet. Both smile, he broadly baring his teeth, she coy and downwardly.

"Hey, M." She gives a little wave and cocks her head to the side. The blonde fringe shimmers in the afternoon sun. Her open mouth, a beautiful abyss, dominates her face when she speaks. She has stopped at a respectable distance, facing M. He is standing overly upright trying to fix her elusive gaze. He steps in closer. "Alright, F?" He nods, almost making a bow as she rotates; hand on neck, repelling him a little. M retreats a step. F opens with an account of her day; she is going to an internet café to contact some friends back home. M, eager not to enter into small talk, knows he must act. Since he had first walked up to F and introduced himself he had yet to get beyond trivial chitchat. A number 2 bus lumbers down the quay, indicating and pulling in at a stop next to where they stand. M grabs F's wrist. "Would you like to jump on this bus and take a round trip of the north side of the city?" She looks at him, both eyes, and smiles, "Sure, let's." Amongst weary schoolchildren, senior citizens and mothers with buggies and bags, M takes F's pink and dainty hand in his and they step onto the bus.

"Two singles, please," M asks. He hands the driver the coins and F her ticket. The bus being crowded, F takes an aisle seat adjacent to a balding, elderly man in an anorak. He looks a moment at her hairdo and clothing and returns to the local newspaper. M sits directly behind F, next to a girl of about twenty in a tracksuit. The bus pulls off across the river as M marvels at the comely curvature of F's head and neck. The shaven back and sides of her hair show a shapely skull, her broad-necked sweater reveals dark and coloured floral tattoos on milky shoulders. The bus begins its ascent. People wait and board; others alight; teenage students in uniform with spots and dyed hair; proud old men in dark suits and caps. All are quiet, subdued, thinking of home's imminent comforts. The local radio broadcasts a jingle; "Playing the hits you can't get out of your head." M thinks of the shit you sometimes can't get out of your head. The track-suited girl next to him sobs into her phone. Her fella has left her. M silently empathises. He leans forward into the aisle pointing the cathedral out to F. They begin to talk; quietly, easily and unselfconsciously. The bus leaves the city centre behind and the incline steepens.

Cold parked cars sheen against cold sunshine. Rows of coloured houses: grey, white, shades of brown, cream and peach stand graduated. They loop, fall, and rise behind well-kept shrubs in small gardens divided by low brick walls or scalped hedges. The bus stops and starts; people come and go. The route is punctuated by intermittent clusters of convenience shops, bars, bookmakers and takeaways. At the old imposing school the old man next to F closes his newspaper and presses the button to signal the bus to stop. F slips into the seat he has vacated. M sits beside her. They look out at a municipal park. Autumn's trees: green, yellow, amber, red, gold, brown and bald filter the sun through the bus's egg-stained Perspex window and onto F's already radiant head. M pays her a compliment. They continue to speak, satisfying their curiosities regarding one another and making little jokes observing the scenes around them. The crowd on the bus thins and they are becoming more and more relaxed together. They are now on a plateau overlooking the city. When they think there is no higher to go the bus takes a left and negotiates another steep hill.

Pebble-dashed, semi-detached houses give way to lace-curtained terraces skirting stark estates. Folks go about their business and gossip outside their homes amid young fellas with tight hair and tracksuits. Muzzled pitbulls and greyhounds walk on patches of wasteland between the estates. Circular scars of scorched earth tell of Halloween's bonfires. They pass the water reservoir against the clear blue sky now reddening. Pigeons and piebalds graze on the football field. All but empty, the bus passes a supermarket, some boarded-up shops, an off-licence and a busy petrol station as it proceeds toward an industrial estate. A telegraph pole adorned with wreaths tells the tale of the victims of last week's car crash. F turns playfully to M and takes a few strands of his long hair. "Can I make you a plait?"

She doesn't wait for his reply. Silently and attentively she begins a narrow French plait behind his ear. He looks ahead, occasionally flitting a glance at her intent, intelligent eyes or her lips pursed in concentration. He sees too her hands; small with nails white and tiny like baby's teeth. They nimble up and down his hair, one overlapping the next, latticing the locks. The odours of the old bus recede. He is surrounded by her fragrance; the movement of her hands, her scent, her face, her hair: all so close he is hypnotised. With all the feeling of an embrace, a warmth rises slowly up his back. Nothing exists, only the sensual moment. F comes in closer and blows a gentle tickle of warm air into his ear. They laugh softly and look intently at one another.

The bus turns around outside a large computer plant. Tired young men and women of many nationalities file onto the bus. Many still wear identity-badges clipped to their clothes. They sit in pairs or alone with their headphones. Production lines, office work, jargon, language-barriers, overtime, shift work, contracts, team building, raises, cuts, promotions, job losses. Finally, they return back downtown to their warm apartments. Soon F and M will be right back where they started. French plait complete, F inspects her handiwork. "You look cool," she says, "do you like it?" "Yes I do, thanks," M replies, meaning it.

The bus continues down the hills, through the estates, past the schools, shops, pubs and chippers. Below, the city is lighting up in anticipation of the dark. F and M are quiet on the way back down. It is a comfortable silence. They reach the cathedral again, lit up and majestic. M takes a slim case from the pocket of his jacket. It rattles a little. Inside is a scarf-pin, some roses he had dried and a note written on the paper that lines the box. It has been waiting in his pocket for a while. "I have a gift for you, thanks for the plait." She makes a practiced blushing downward-eye and shoulder-shrug and gently takes the case, "Thank you", the big mouth tries to sneak a smile as she tucks away the gift.

Another number 2 perpetuates the cycle back up the hills of the north side. M and F are soon back to where they started. Outside a window displaying garish homewares they stand a moment on the footpath. The spell is nearly broken. "I enjoyed our journey together, bye-bye," was all that she said. He; stunned by the brush of a brief, sweet, kiss from her lips to his, remained mute.

M sat in the bath that night. He was regarding his hairy, sudsy knees. He listened to the drain guzzle and gargle the water away. Hot water sank and steam rose around him in the chill bathroom air. He looked down waiting for his feet to appear. When all of the water had gone he was still staring down at his toes, twiddling the tidy plait in his hair.

F took some vegetables and a packet of pulses from her bag and placed them on the kitchen counter. She took out the cigar-case and secreted it away. She started to prepare the meal and texted her boyfriend to meet him for a beer while they waited for the lentils to stew. It was cold and she put

## Home

on a jacket and scarf. "That's a nice pin on your scarf," commented her boyfriend on the way home. "Thanks, I got it in a charity shop today," was her answer.

That's all. F went home. She still wears the pin from time to time.

Me, I wore the plait in my hair for as long as it stayed and still jump on the number 2 every now and again.

*Paul Lewis*
*Cork and Galway*

## Simple Quietude

You can feed me
crusty bread,
garlic olives
and tuna salad
and I will be fulfilled,
lounging in the armchair
by the balcony door,
illuminated by the last rays,
skin shiny,
scented with lotion,
flip-flop dangling,
book in hand
as I catch the light
in your eyes.

Sipping tea,
you smile,
content in the shadows,
puzzling over the crossword
from last week's newspaper.

Becalmed
in light and shade,
we sit in silent symmetry
at the hour before umbra
in Los Gigantos.

*Máire Morrissey-Cummins*
*Greystones, Co. Wicklow*

---

*(Umbra: The darkest part of a shadow cast by the Moon, Sun or another body during an eclipse.)*

*Home*

## Llewyn Davis, Bringing It All Back Home

There were ghosts on the film screen
and ghosts in the audience.

Afterwards, in a nearby bar
we strangers reminisce
when the world was almost new,
adventures we had,
great ones we met –
none of us knowing
if we were speaking the truth
or telling fishing stories
we had reason to believe.

Oh that night we drank with Phil Ochs
could have been that we saw him
step from a bar and into a cab, positively
at West 4th and West 10th Streets.
Beer and marijuana had the best of us
as we circled back to that corner
again and again
and again.

Decades later, lines from songs
and questions keep circling –
were we ever there,
where have we gone,
and what wings will carry us
as we try to find our way home?

*Tim Dwyer*
*New York, United States*

# Tom

I've gone and broke the spine
of *The Tibetan Book of Living and Dying*

Facebook tagged you in Sligo
and for that second, that fraction of—

well I thought you were alive
and bawled at the good of it all

me, here making shite of books about dying
you, there – warming your bodhrán.

*Niamh Boyce*
*Athy*

*Home*

## Murphy, Portmarnock Strand

*Kate Quigley*
*Przylep, Poland*

## Saint, Sea and the Cyclops of Tory Island

Gentle saint, powerful,
daughter of the North
washed ashore with sailors
by the lighthouse,
now in your grave
of holy clay
protecting seamen.

Do you hear her
crying on the wind?
Her three baby sons
flung into the fuming waves
by her jealous father.
His death at their hands foretold.

Does the one-eyed seer
ever rest, war weary,
in his cathedral of birdsong,
and mourn their loss?

Or does he, in his fury,
still claw the granite cliffs,
streak them red with his blood,
rip the land bridge that divides you?

Does he, Balor,
ferocious cyclops,
still battle encroaching waves
as the intransigent sea erodes,
triumphantly
trashing foam into sea caves,
gouging craters?

*Anne Irwin*
*Rockfield Park, Co. Galway*

## Teeth

This house has grown teeth. They certainly weren't here when I moved in last year. I know that for a fact because I paid an engineer good money to give it the once-over. And that man was thorough. The sort that wouldn't blink an eye at slithering down a drain or shooting up a loft, iPod in one hand, lump hammer in the other. At the time, he pointed out a missing tile or two, a few plaster cracks, the need for a lick of paint. But teeth? Definitely no mention of teeth. He zipped around the house like a forensic scientist, banging on walls, pipes, fittings. Not a crooked thumbtack holding up a gas arrears bill on the underside of the antique pine corner-unit escaped his beady eye. Definitely no pearlies.

They're here now. I hear them at night. Grinding. Like the sound of sabres sharpening up for a showdown. I lie in bed imagining canines lengthening by the minute and I drift off to a jungle – alligators everywhere snapping off legs, arms, even heads; farther south to where starving dingoes, capable of finishing off a writer in one sitting, lie in wait.

You don't expect your house to have teeth, like some evolutionary aberrant, some mutant with the slimmest chance of driving progress. I'm sick of it. I called my dentist out for a home visit. It cost a fortune and he refused to do a goddamn thing about the chompers. Said I should go visit a head doctor. But what does a head doctor know about teeth?

*Maureen Gallagher*
*Galway*

## Darkness Is the Absence

I am a scoop of ice cream,
melting into this broken chair,
the dark summer heat
drying me out
like the contents of every
plate, bowl, glass and cup
I've seen fit to leave
lying
in this place.

*Dean Buckley*
*West of Here*

Home

## Our Downstairs Landlady's Request to My Mother, London NW 7, 1969

If you're passing the Co-op please bring me:
a small grapefruit and something for a sore foot;

The *Daily Express* and a rusty forceps;
a box of Brillo pads and the cheapest

dentist's drill they have; as many dried prunes
as you can manage and a pair of support tights

with a hole blown in them; a nose hair scissors
and half a jar of beetroot; one kipper

and a lorry load of toilet roll.
A gallon of weed killer and bag of kidney stones.

One tin of fish paste and botulism
soup. A comic book for your boy,

which, when I give it to him, I'll say is something
you could never afford. A personality even

more disgusting than mine, which you'll find
between the meat pies and stuff

for unclogging drains. If you're passing the Co-op
which you must if you want to get back here

from where you're going. I'll pay you Friday,
when I collect my pension. Remind me.

*Kevin Higgins*
*Galway City*

Aisling Christian Bookshop
Lower Abbeygate Street
(Opposite Oxfam)

Sub-City Comics Galway is centrally located in the heart of Galway city. With a huge selection of Graphic Novels, and weekly deliveries of American Comics we also cater for speciality orders. We stock Collectors Card Games such as Magic, Yu-Gi-Oh!, Match Attax, Slam Attax and Pokemon. You will also find Action Figures, Board Games and statues as well as T-shirts and posters. Definitley something for everyone, and if we don't have what you're looking for we will gladly order it for you.
We will also gladly post out your orders to people who just make it into our shop.

SubCity Dublin
2 Exchequer Street,
Temple Bar, Dublin
01 - 677 1902

SubCity Galway
Corbetts Ct.,
Eyre Square, Galway
091 - 565994

New & Second-Hand Books

Specialising in Bibles, Devotional, Theological, Apologetical, Children's books,
Wide selection of Cards

Opening hours
Mon – Sat   10 am – 6:00 pm

# Seafood Restaurant & Traditional Fish & Chips Quay Street Galway

www.mcdonaghs.net

*Home*

## Octopus Still Growing, Fleeing Visitors Warn

My eccentricities are expanding
Do they grow to fill a space?
Purple tentacles, uncurling
I'd better say I almost see them
Twisting and twirling all over the place.

Sometimes they come bumping
Right up to someone else's face
It's too late to whip them back
They're so long and wild
Do they grow to fill a space?

My eccentricities are expanding
The more room around me the bigger their size
I see my reflection in the neighbours
A troubling shadow
In their lychee-soft eyes.

My eccentricities are expanding
I used to keep them so under control
Clamped in armpits, tangled 'round hair
Or stuffed in boots
Next to my sole.

Back when I used to live in town
And was always, always on the puke-green **Dart**
Never more than an arm's reach from anyone
A couple of feet
Rattling along in the dark.

I'd sit and fake being lost in a book
Hold it up to my nose
To hide them, to keep them
From reaching and dancing
I dreaded them mirrored in the sealed windows.

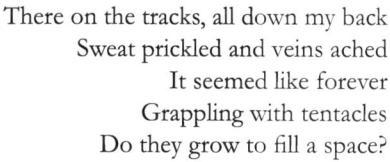

## ROPES 2014

There on the tracks, all down my back
Sweat prickled and veins ached
It seemed like forever
Grappling with tentacles
Do they grow to fill a space?

My eccentricities are expanding
But here, where the lake is rough
They stretch, they flex, they remind me
How they used to barely live
But now I think they're living too much.

Here is where they've broken out
I catch them swinging on the washing line
Or off singing in the compost heap
Throwing bottles around
At breakfast time.

In the shop, or at the school
I'm blurting words out, inkily
The heavy tendrils writhe and squirm
They're massive and muscular
And magnificent, really.

Though sometimes they drag and trip me up
And I wish they'd disappear
When they're suckering
And spittling slime and ink
And words no one wants to hear.

But then at least they don't mind who's looking
When they're swelling full and odd
And a lot of the time I'm carried
Up in the clouds
In the tickle of a giant cephalopod.

They're coiled around me, languidly
My secret arms that have escaped

*Home*

Here they thrive
Better out than in
Do they grow to fill a space?

*Jessamine O Connor*
*Blown In To Sligo*

*Artwork* **Octopus** *by*

*Rebecca Connell*
*Galway*

## On the Hill there Is a Tree

For as long as I can remember, the people of the village have come to whisper their secrets to me. My roots stretch down past the millipedes and the stench of damp, past the buried and forgotten things: treasures lost, stones that once were castles and the bones of saints and liars and cowards. So I am strong enough to carry their burdens. I want them to let their secrets out so they won't weigh heavy on their hearts, weaken their bones, fester and rot. They speak into my sticky tree-knot, as is the way, and then they retreat to the village down the hill – their steps assured, their shoulders lighter, their breaths deep and even.

But now I am old and their whisperings have grown loud and constant as the wind through my branches. So I tried to unburden myself a little. I offered the secrets to the soil with my roots, but the earth contains the secrets of the dead and has no space for those of the living. I tried to give the secrets to the breeze. It whispers to me, but when I whispered back, it would not listen. I whistled the secrets to the birds that nested in my branches, but they could not understand my language. And now the secrets have made me heavy. They may come with axes soon. When they chop me down, I do not know what will happen to the secrets. They may flow from me like blood or scatter and dance on the wind.

There is a girl in the village who does not skip or whistle or sing. She knows secrets too, but she does not know that she knows. Her name is Wendy and she visits me often, lumbering up the hill with a cake box from the bakery. "Wendy's off to beg for scraps like a dog," her half-sisters tease when Wendy slinks out of the house. The baker was friends with her father and he often gives her the little cakes that have not quite risen, the pastries with misshapen fruit, the blackened heel of a crusty loaf. She devours it all but it is never enough. If I could speak, I would tell Wendy that it is not hunger that she feels in her stomach, but fear, and no amount of food can unfrighten a person.

I am Wendy's only friend and she mine, although I cannot tell her this. She sits on the mossy ground and whispers into my knot and tells me everything:

"Father is starting to fade and I'm worried he will disappear. I searched the house for a photograph but they were all missing. When I asked Mother about it, she grew angry and said 'I'm busy now, Wendy.' If I close my eyes and focus hard, I can see him. The sun is behind him so I can't make out his face, but somehow I still know that he's smiling. I'm trying to hold on to these memories, to keep some part of him with me. I remember how small my hand was in his and the gold ring he wore with the onyx stone, black as a pupil. They say he was a thief, that he stole money from the church before he disappeared. I hear them but it's like they're talking about someone else. I don't know why he left or why he didn't say goodbye. Maybe I did something wrong. I am always wrong."

Wendy's mother and stepfather drink in the village every evening and leave her at home to watch her three younger half-sisters who delight in tormenting her. No one would believe this of Lily, Rose and Dahlia; with their fair skin, blonde hair in ringlets and sweet smiles for everyone. The people of the village call the three sisters *The Blossoms*, and in turn, the three sisters call Wendy *The Weed*. Wendy fears sleep. This is her secret, a shameful thing for a girl of her age. She dreams of wolves in the long grass and caged birds that refuse to sing. On the edges, some terrible thing is worming its way into the light, closer and closer, and she will not allow it to take shape. So, late at night, once her mother and stepfather have stumbled home to bed and her half-sisters are asleep, she walks through the town and up the hill where she used to walk with her father many years ago and she sits and whispers to me.

She told me about the pet bird her mother bought for her sister Rose. When the bird would not talk, Rose lost interest in that creature straight away, so Wendy was the one who gave the bird its water and food, even though it upset her to see it there in its little cage, flapping its wings but never taking flight.

"Bird, hello, bird," Wendy said as she cleaned its cage.

Then one day the bird answered back: "Wendy, hello, Wendy."

"Oh!" said Wendy, and she called Rose and told her the bird had talked.

Rose peered at the bird through the metal bars. "Say 'hello', bird."

"Wendy, hello, Wendy," said the bird.

Rose tapped her fingers on the cage. "No, bird, say 'hello, Rose'."

"Wendy, hello, Wendy," said the bird.

"It's *my* bird! It should say *my* name." Rose opened the door and stuck her hand into the cage as the bird squawked and retreated. She clasped it in her hand and withdrew it from the cage. "There now. Say 'Rose… Rose… Rose…'" she repeated, her voice growing louder with each command.

"Rose, let it go." Wendy reached out her hand, but Rose's grip tightened around the bird.

"No, it's *mine!*" She shouted and snatched the bird from Wendy's grasp. Rose stopped then and was still. She unclenched her hand and looked down at the unmoving creature. "It's dead," she said. "You killed it, Weed. You killed it."

Wendy sobbed as she told me this and crammed another lopsided cake into her mouth.

"Rose is holding a funeral for the bird today in the pasture behind our house. She has invited all of the village and Father Steel has even agreed to say some prayers. Mother has bought Rose a new black dress and black velvet ribbons for Dahlia and Lily to tie around their curls. Rose told everyone that I killed the bird. She said she didn't blame me, that it wasn't my fault I was so clumsy. I know I didn't kill the bird, but nobody would believe me anyway. I must go now to the funeral. Goodbye, tree."

I was lonely when she left so I stretched my roots as far as I could, down the hill to the pasture. I saw her standing off to the side, biting her nails as the villagers cast sympathetic glances at The Blossoms. "Such a sensitive child," they said as they smiled at Rose who sniffed and dabbed her eyes with a lace handkerchief, a perfect picture of mourning. She was flanked on each side by Dahlia and Lily, who patted her shoulder and threw daggered looks at Wendy, who looked at her shoes. They had fashioned a tiny coffin for the bird out of an old shoebox, and they lowered it into the hole in the ground as Father Steel recited a prayer. This was the moment I chose. I summoned up the last of my strength and pushed my roots up as far as they could reach. I made the earth shake. I did it for Wendy. The villagers stepped back and gasped as the earth peeled back in clumps. I pushed that terrible secret to the surface. They saw the onyx ring on that skeletal hand.

The baker looked to Wendy's mother. "But… that's… that's his ring…"

Wendy looked at her mother and stepfather. They had stepped back, their mouths agape. Her stepfather's face had turned ashen. "God forgive us," he muttered. "God forgive us…" over and over again. Wendy looked from her stepfather to her mother and that terrible knowledge that had always been there finally came to light. The Blossoms were crying for real then, bewildered tears. Wendy stepped backwards and turned and ran to me.

They came with axes as I knew they would. They traced my roots and saw that it was I who had revealed the secret to them. I did not blame them when I saw the mob coming up the hill. They cannot help but turn on those who know their secrets. Unburdened by that weight, they are burdened anew by the knowledge that they have handed over the very weapon that could destroy them. I have seen it again and again. I know how suddenly lovers can become enemies, or families spill the blood that they share.

"This tree is possessed!" shouted Father Steel. "I will cast out this demon." He uttered frantic prayers and moved about my trunk. He sprinkled holy water on me, a drizzle I couldn't feel. Wendy's mother and stepfather searched for her in the crowd. They told The Blossoms to find her. The girls were still weeping, dazed, as they made their way around the group, asking the villagers if they had seen Wendy. Everyone shook their heads, no, and turned back to the priest, who was bellowing at the makeshift congregation on the hill.

"We must take action!" Father Steel signalled for the men with axes to approach. "Chop it down. Chop it into pieces and then we will make a bonfire. We will rid ourselves of this unholy thing!"

Wendy's mother and stepfather continued to search for her, but they could not find her because she was perched in my branches. Wendy became a bird. I saw it happen. Set free by truth, filled with crystal light, baptised by gentle rain – she became the prettiest bird that nobody could cage, with feathers of colours that only exist in dreams. Her song was sweeter than anything known to man. Every time they struck my bark with one of their axes, they stopped and marvelled as Wendy sang out one of their secrets:

"Rose killed the bird. She crushed its tiny heart. Rose killed the bird…

"Father Steel stole. He stole the collection money. Father Steel stole…"

I whispered the secrets to her and she sang them out and set them free until the villagers backed away. They retreated down the hill and returned to the village where they remained. We looked down as they made their way back into their homes. They did not speak of what had happened.

Night set in. From up on the hill we could see candles dotted about in the windows of the houses below. Pinpricks of orange and yellow in the blackness. They offered soft light, some comfort here or there, but darkness seeped in at the edges.

"Wendy, hello, Wendy," I said, as Wendy sang and sang.

*Máire T. Robinson*
*Dublin*

Home

## Family Vault

I tell the children
I own half the house;
their father will buy me out.

*Which half?*
they ask.

I own the smoky smell of grilling ham
basted with brown sugar,
honey and mustard,

the embrace of the couch,
where breastfed babies
lolled,

the book shelves,
now host to holiday trinkets,
photos that happened since;

the child's courage
as she finds her path
away from danger,

the daffodils in April,
cherry blossoms in May,

the ghost that in my voice
comforts the troubled child
back to sleep,

the smell of me
that wafts out
from pockets of trapped air,

the look of reproach
in the children's eyes,

when he breaks some tradition
dear to them,

the echo of a reply
I always gave
when he teased them
in that playful way.

All the renovations he will do,
I'll still be there.

*Aideen Henry*
*Claddagh, Co. Galway*

# Home

## There Are Two Ways

After dinner one time, Moo said there are two ways to get through life – you pray or you laugh. Ricky and I certainly didn't pray, but things weren't really funny so we didn't laugh much either. It didn't matter because Moo was wrong about all that. You can just breathe and breathe and get through life without any praying or laughing. That's what she did in her last few months anyway.

After the funeral, Dad said there are two ways to deal with someone's death – you hold on or you let go. We weren't sure which way he was recommending. He was always bad at talking to us about hard things and we felt bad for him so we just nodded like we knew, like we really knew. We didn't know. All we knew was that by the time school got out for the summer, Dad had a girlfriend named Marcia.

After Marcia moved in, she said there are two ways to live with other people – be close or be distant. This was right after she instituted the first Fish and Checkers Friday, which both Ricky and I missed. When we missed Mac and Parcheesi Monday, she told Dad we weren't dealing with the loss well and needed to see someone. We missed F&C Friday because we were mowing the Smiths', Georges' and Maloneys' lawns and we missed M&P Monday because we were using our earnings to buy a bugging device, which is how we heard Marcia's laments on our emotional well-being.

After we were late to our first session, Dr Bob Guardiola said there are two ways to handle change – but before he could tell us what they were, Ricky started choking on his granola bar and I pretended I didn't know he was faking and started bawling big, wet tears. Ricky says I'm one of the best fake criers there is. I just go into this zone where nothing exists except me and my tears. When Dad picked us up and saw my puffy face, he said that was enough therapy. Marcia and him got in a big fight that night and I think he got mad at us for making the couch into a bed for him before they were even finished. When school started back up, Dad signed us up for cross country, which he insisted was not punishment.

After our first two-mile run with the team, Coach P said there are two ways to deal with shin splints – rub them in or rub them out. We quit the next day, which Marcia was cool with because she never thought we'd stick with it anyway. She said what we needed was more family and so she sent us to her mom's condo after school.

After we met Marlene and planted a micro-camera in her kitchen, she

said there are two ways to deal with Marcia – booze or earplugs. Then she said booze *and* earplugs. Then she put in some earplugs and started drinking red wine out of a plastic souvenir cup. She was asleep on the couch, drooling, when Dad and Marcia picked us up later. Dad let out a big sigh and Marcia's cheeks turned pink as strawberry ice cream, which we got later, on account of their combined guilt.

After we got home, Ricky said there are two ways to live – get rich or die trying. He had been listening to a lot of 50 Cent lately. He said mowing lawns wasn't enough money for what he wanted, but he didn't say what it was he wanted. He stuffed some clothes into a backpack and told me not to worry because he'd be sending postcards where he was going. I asked him if he had stamps and, knowing the answer was no, I snuck into Dad's office to get some. When I got back to his room, he was gone.

After Marcia called the cops, Officer Levin said there are only two ways to handle a missing child situation – stay by the phone or go looking. Dad said that was bullshit, there were a million ways to handle it: they could call his friends, they could talk to the bus company, they could print posters and pass them out. Suddenly, Dad was full of ideas like I'd never seen him, billboards, group walks, neighbor interviews, radio announcements. Officer Levin told him to calm down. While they were bickering, I slipped out the back door. At first I just sat on the porch and pretend-smoked invisible cigarettes because no matter how much cancer they cause, they still look so cool. I remembered Moo sitting on the porch and smoking in the dead of winter like it was nothing. Even though it was cold and she was my mom, she looked so powerful. So I pretend-smoked a few cigarettes, smashing the old ones under my foot like no-good ants, until I realized I was late to mow the Smiths' lawn and left. They asked where Ricky was and I said he was sick and they said to tell him to feel better. I said I would and kept mowing. When I finished, they paid me in cash because, really, that's the only way.

*Brooke Randel*
*Philadelphia, United States*

*Home*

# Home for Christmas

*ROPES 2014*

*Kate Quigley*
*Przylep, Poland*

*Home*

## Armageddon and Rusheen Bay

Down a winding road past Bearna
where the dry, stone wall fades into sea,
clumps of wiry grass
on sodden turf enclose a cove.
There on a low tide
a flight of swallows
coach their young
to soar on command,
swirl, drop, and soar again,
'til together, as one,
they fly to Africa.

My boy has flown.
He is in Saigon.
None of his friends are at home.
We have sacrificed our children
to the narcissism of bankers.

The swallows will return to their nests
in the eaves and barns of our countryside.

What will happen to our children?

*Anne Irwin*
*Rockfield Park, Co. Galway*

## Not

You not here
to not know what
key goes in what lock;
to tell not exactly the truth
about who said what to whom;
to spend the whole first day
of the January sales
examining tea towels
you end up not buying; to notice
I've not yet mowed the lawn,
to not know when
the oil will run out, or have
a plan B, or a good word
for your enemies; to send me out
at four in the morning in search of
cigarettes; to stand smoking
by the kitchen window and say
*this didn't happen*; to smirk
and tell the world
*moving furniture was never his thing,*
the day I do my shoulder in
carrying your coffin.

*Kevin Higgins*
*Galway City*

*Home*

# The Sugarloaf Mountain, Co. Wicklow, Ireland

*Máire Morrissey-Cummins*
*Greystones, Co. Wicklow*

## To the Second Born
*For my younger sister Gillian*

I'm the unwitting pioneer
in the liquid darkness,
but I can leave few beacons
to guide your voyage.
You are the wary follower
on an expedition I did not plan.
You will sail an ocean I cannot chart.

I whisper to you from an unformed throat,
record words in braille on birthing muscle,
words you will read with translucent fingertips,
inscribing them in the whorls of your thumbs.

Silently, you'll nod and you'll remember,
grow wise with the experiences of another,
gather the strength to break
the template that formed your sister,
summon the courage to plot
your own course through
strange, amniotic waters.


*Ruth Quinlan*
*Tralee, Co. Kerry*

## What Sarah Knows

Sarah is pocket-sized for an eight-year-old and can barely reach the table. Still she presses the good cutlery down with extra care, spits on them, rubs them with the end of the half-clean tea towel, shines them 'til they look like silver. It's a trick learnt from Popeye. If she could be a sailor, she would, but it seems like sailors need to have loud voices. They need to be tall and strong too, and for that she needs vegetables. Sarah knows she will never have a loud voice, so she has decided to be a detective. She'd still like to be tall and strong, though, so she's working on eating more vegetables. Gerry and her Mam don't agree with her: they think it's a conspiracy by the food companies and buy most of their food from the frozen section. Sarah spends all her pocket money on spinach.

"What the fuck are ye doing with the good forks?"
*Silence as Sarah pushes her fringe to stop it falling in her eyes.*
"Don't you know yer not s'posed to be messing around in me drawers?"
*Silence as she shuffles her weight onto the other foot.*
"And who do ye thinks going to have to clean this shit up, when yer off in school learning yer fancy fucking sums?"
*Silence as she chews the inside of her cheek.*
"Nothing to say fer yerself, come ere Jenny, come look what she's done now, put a sheet on the table and all, like some kinda fucking gypsy."
Silence as she looks at the floor.
"Jenny?"
"Will ye just bring her to school, sure don't ye know she hasn't a clue, it's not her fault, her daddy was a bleedin' headcase," Sarah's mother replies.

*I've got a clue; I know lots of things: I know that the sun sets everyday. I know that spinach will make me strong enough to punch Gerry and Mam so I can run away with Kevin. I know that the flowers I put on the table are daisies. If they keep cursing like this they are going straight to Hell. I can't tell anyone the truth or I'll get locked up for compulsive lying like Da.*

Sarah is making a list in wobbly writing in the back seat of Gerry's battered Fiat. She sits wedged between his football gear and a cardboard box full of alarms from his latest business investment. When she's not listing she picks crumbs of Pop-Tart from the seat and flicks them at Gerry. He is breaking all the rules of the road; she's been counting. They watched a video in school with hedgehogs that showed them what you couldn't do. Then she found a book in the library and double-checked because hedgehogs didn't seem like a reliable source.

She hadn't wanted to find out she was living with criminals but there it was in black and white, a list of all the Rules of the Road. Today they've endangered three cyclists by driving too close to the curb, broken a pedestrian crossing, and gone too fast through an orange light. She's got three weeks' worth of notes and is seriously considering turning them in to the guards. The hedgehogs said more and more people are dying on the roads, so withholding evidence would make her an accomplice and she needs a clean record if she's going to ever become a detective. She's glad her Mam watches Law and Order or she wouldn't have had a clue.

"Will ye stop dilly-dallying and get yer dumb arse out of the car?"
*Silence as she scrapes the zip on her jacket along the side of the car*

Sarah doesn't pay attention in class. She doesn't like the baby books they read, or the fact that the teacher talks in a slow voice. She doesn't care if Huggy Bear has a new pair of shoes, or who has the neatest handwriting, or if some kid peed their pants at small break. Sarah likes sneaking around at lunch; she tests herself. Last week she stole thirty packets of crisps from lunchboxes undetected, and was a bit annoyed when they were found in the computer press and Colm got all the credit.

It especially annoys her when the teacher talks extra slow to her. Sarah scribbles pictures of bananas instead of answers in her textbooks. Spelling tests are the worst:

"Spell horse, now, Sarah. That's the kind of horse that goes 'neigh'."
*Silence as she rolls her pencil between her fingers.*

Sarah loves words. It took her ages to Google the ones that sound the same but mean different things. Her teacher wasn't impressed when she wrote "deer/dear." Said she should pay more attention to her spelling list so she'd know which one to write.

"Ok, everyone, have you got that one? Ok, Sarah, you too; just nod and let me know."

# Home

*Silence as she keeps her head down, writes "HOARSE" in block capitals.*

Then there's resource teaching, where the special kids go for a few hours. Connor licks the table and Carl throws things at the floor. There's an alphabet on the wall in lurid colours. They get to fill in the blanks in sentences for hours on end. Sarah tried getting out, but she wouldn't do the signs with her hands so they made her stay. Said she must be deaf, maybe, or stupid.

They tested her ears: told her to raise her hand when she heard the beep. She didn't like the way they spoke to her so she let the sound get louder and louder. There was a special ear doctor after and her Mam spent three days crying.

"What did I fucking do to deserve her; I can't afford this shit. I just can't handle it, Gerry, hearing aids, on top of everything else. Next thing she'll need bleedin' glasses."

Gerry sent Sarah to her room that night and brought her Mam out for dinner in a fancy restaurant. When they came back she could hear the banging and screaming and laughing in their cardboard house until two in the morning. Sarah wished she needed hearing aids then.

Sarah just finished reading a book about Brownies. The book was about two kids in a house full of fighting. Then they'd heard a rumour about Brownie's that could fix everything. All they did was make everything nice and ready in the morning and the shouting stopped. That's why she got up at seven and made the table. It took her two hours to find the flowers and make a table cloth. She'd used the nicest sheet. Sarah had thought it would work; she'd even run the idea by Kevin. She's thinking of writing a letter of complaint about false promises.

Gerry broke a glass last night. That had been the worst part to clean up this morning. Sarah didn't want him to remember that he broke it, or why. He'd been so angry about the sheet on the table that she'd hidden the cut on her hand. She is still hiding it because the other kids would think she was even thicker if they saw her hand wrapped in bloodied toilet paper. She's tucked it inside her cardigan sleeve and is writing with the wrong hand. The Brownie idea hadn't worked. She'd left the book on the newspaper pile so maybe Mam would read it and get the idea.

"Are ye always the last out of school?"
*Silence as she slots herself into the backseat and fixes her seatbelt*

"Jesus Christ, can't even be nice to ye, like talking to a bleedin' wall."
*Silence as she stares past him out the window.*

Sarah makes note of the curse words on page three of her notebook. That's seventy-two bad words this week. She's making note in case God loses count. She'll appeal the decision; she has to be sure Gerry will go to Hell. It's her favourite part of the day. Home time, which means they send her outside so they can have some alone time. Sarah doesn't mind as it means she gets to see Kevin. She goes to the place where the world stops speaking. At the end of the hedgerow she's dug a tunnel, her size only. She's got a space in there, a small, dry, flat patch hollowed out in the centre of their hedge. She has stones in a small circle and sticks for a fire. She never lights it, but she feels its warmth anyway. There's an old paint can hanging on a branch that she stirs from time to time. She waits for Kevin. Kevin can't speak either and that's why she likes him. They sit in silence together. Sometimes she reads and he nestles on her shoulder.

"Sarah, get the fuck inside. It's dinner time, away with the fairies as per bleedin' usual."
*Silence as she slowly closes her book*
"I give up."
*Silence as she picks up a twig and snaps it.*

She presses her lips to the top of Kevin's head and leaves him spinach that she's had tucked in her pocket since yesterday's dinner. He'll need his strength when they run away. Sarah thinks how Kevin's just a squirrel and she's just dumb. But dumb doesn't mean you're stupid. So she reminds herself that she knows things:

I know the day is nearly over. I know that the washing-up won't be that big because it's Gerry's night to cook, which means pizza. I know that fabric softener doesn't clean things no matter what Mam says. I know that the police address is two traffic lights after my house and on your right, that detectives are good at figuring things out, taking notes, and being silent, and I'm the quietest person I know.

*Alvy Carragher*
*Wherever My Family*

*Home*

## The Move

We dumped it all in
Shards of childhood
Adolescent frowns and
Cheap laughs
The heavy waste of time weighed the rusting skip
Several memories whistled in the breeze
While lighter moments whirled through crevices.
I threw the last of the harsh words in
The sudden release tripped my footing
I pricked my finger on the rust
It bled maroon and gave a beautiful warmth
To the cold morning.
You gave me an old caring look from years ago
I was surprised you remembered it
But then the curdling smell
Of our collection dampened the moment
An odd liquid oozed and glistened on the metal frame
It was time to let this drip alone and dry.
I left
Warm from the pulse in my wound.

*Rachael Hanaphy-Pigott*
*Dublin*

Domestic * Industrial * Commercial
Agricultural

C2 Registered & VAT Registered

Graigue, Rathcabbin, Roscrea,
Co. Tipperary.

Ph: 057 91 39107 - 087 16773522

Arts & Science Building, NUI, Galway
Tel: 091-492350  Fax: 091-494571
Email: printthat@nuigalway.ie
www.nuigalway.ie/printthat

Located ON CAMPUS in NUI GALWAY

graphic design . photocopying . brochures .
binding . books . large format . posters . flyers
. laminating . tickets . typing . business cards .
stationery . letterheads . cd/dvd duplication .
compliment slips . signage .

## The University Bookshop

Under the Library,
beside the Restaurant

For all your text books

Specialist books to order

Excellent service and
friendly staff!

University Switchboard:
(091) 524 411, Ext. 2590
Direct Tel.: (091) 525 318
Fax: (091) 527 742

## OÉ Gaillimh
## NUI Galway

**French Studies**
**School of Languages, Literatures and Cultures**

• 1-year taught MA in French. A combination of seminars, translation studies and research. Seminars include translation and among others: Autofiction, Critical Approaches and Methods, Literature of France in Algeria and Representations of the Islamic Other in Medieval France.
• 1-year taught MA in Translation Studies with French and another language. This interdisciplinary programme investigates the centrality of the practice and process of translation to society, history and culture, and the crucial importance of translation in contemporary critical debates. Students select two languages from French, Spanish, Italian and German.
• 1-year taught MA in Advanced Language Skills. This programme (for students whose first language is English, French, German, Italian or Spanish, and who are competent in at least one of the others), is designed to provide advanced linguistic and technical training to prepare linguists for careers in several areas of specialised language.
• MLitt/PhD in French and Francophone studies.

For more detailed information see: www.nuigalway.ie/french
For graduate studies enquiries, email: french@nuigalway.ie
or contact Ms Emer O'Flynn, tel: + 353 (0) 91 492397, fax: + 353 (0) 91 494508
Address: French Studies, School of Languages, Literatures and Cultures,
National University of Ireland, Galway, Ireland

*Home*

## Kids in School

Stop the lights, I want to get out
for a walk, to talk,
for a cup of tea, to breathe.

Stop the ride, I want to get off
to dye my hair, to paint my nails,
to think, to drink.

Turn off the noise.
No crying or screaming.
No teaching or preaching.
No coaxing or feeding.
No washing or shopping.
No cooking or cleaning.
The kids self-sufficient
is all that I want.

*Rewind* the tape.
Turn *back* the clock.
Turn *up* the noise.
I'm cracking up.
My teaspoon's echoing in my cup.

Rooms seem bare.
I sit and stare
at lonely toys
on tidy shelves;
life is empty
since they've left.

Faye Boland
Kenmare, Co. Kerry

## They Sold Their Calves in Spring

They remind me of a chain gang, taking their shuffling half-steps to the altar. They always have. I wait, picking my moment to stand up, joining the retreating communion line and the priest bellowing, "Body of Christ."
 Everyone notices. The old men in the nave, old teachers, old exes, neighbours, and mothers pulling their children off the pews in front like they have grappling hooks for hands. I dart out, starting to shiver on this summer's day, thinking the worst is over, but of course it's not. There are people lining the porch, the church steps, the car park. I must pass the hundreds who came for him, came to see him off.
 I walk back through the village as we used to, he and I, every Sunday morning growing up. We'd leave right after communion to be back in time to open the shop. Granddad would brush a hand over whatever was growing through the roadside fence: the wild carrot sprouting, fuchsia withering, foxgloves bitten by frost. "Look," he'd say, "the mountain streams are swollen from the Saturday night rain; toss them, those sycamore helicopters, into the sky, see whose goes the highest." Today there was no rush to open, not when he was a half hour from being planted, like an oversized root, in Rosshill Yard. Expectations rest easy on the dead.
 I opened up anyway. I knew no one would come, the entire village and its mother was funnelled into the funeral mass. It was my great-grandfather who'd bought the site, but Granddad who'd given the shop its wings to fly through recession after recession and come out the other side. It's the type of place you can buy your half pound of ham, your gluten-free bread, your drum of gas and masking tape. You may find tights next to mop heads, and rat poison hugging the Listerine.
 I stood leaning on the outside of the counter in my funeral suit. Newsprint darkened my fingers like a new set of prints but instead of giving a new identity, it was like recovering one. It's funny, the things you miss. The papers were a few days old. Nobody had thought to clear them, too busy with arrangements. I flicked through them; from sports to horoscopes to murders, new figures of the unemployed and emigrated. Still shivering – trying to remember how to keep a body in this low, western heat – I had the door open, looking out on the empty streets of the village. The sun caught the red paint on the wooden door, flaked from Atlantic weather. A soft crimson, like the soil I'd left abroad, sunshine like the heat of an open peat stove; it now seemed it was dreamt. I'd been on to my mother about

putting in automatic doors but she wouldn't have it. Her and the finances both, I suppose.

Growing up having a shop attached to your house had its ups-and-downs. You were almost destined to lose the fight against Nestlé and Cadbury. You were pestered in school to sort out lads with smokes. You had the whole parish to raise you from your front room. I could see them too, the generations walking through those red doors. The ones I'd liked most were nearly all dead, all the old characters. The rest I had seen at the wake: shaking hands, kissing cheeks, drinking my mother's tea that some local woman assigned herself to make.

All those people, I had learned their names off long ago, standing inside the counter on a Wednesday when the *Connacht Tribune* came in, Granddad at the till, standing over me, asking me to hand out the papers he'd marked and put aside for people. With print on my fingers, I was there with him, a boy again. He'd close up for the night and test me as we took in the cash, emptying the tills of their miniature mounds of gold horses, silver salmons and stags.

"Who got the *Connachts?*"

"Mrs Hopkins, Padraig Molloy, Mary Lydon, Sean Pierce, John Joe Walsh," the long list began.

"*The Indo?*"

*The Star. The Sun. The Times. The Farmers Journal.* These names scrawled atop newspapers that we kept and then sighed over if nobody showed to collect them, when we hadn't seen them for days, like they'd forgotten we were here. But they remembered to come and be seen standing over my Granddad's open coffin. I'd left my mother to fend off the questions when they started.

"What stage is your lad at now?"

"Did he pass the driving test the second time?"

"Has he found a job out there yet, has he?"

They read my life off my mother as if catching up on the soap section of the *RTÉ Guide.* Some things are harder to forget, but gossip has a distinctive melody. I had returned to this village version of myself, the part sown and preened within these walls and behind these two old tills.

Out the door are the familiar chimneys, smoking year-round, the church steeple, the bridge and portions of sky taken by the mountains as their own. A village devoid of noise. There was only one pub open now, the flower boxes less vibrant than when I'd left; the post office door was losing its green, like ours was losing its red, to the weather. We should have placed bets: 10/1 on who'd be next to go under in a country of locked-up doors. It was only a matter of time before the tourists passed through this very village, camera ready for their scenic drive through Connemara, just to lower their lenses and drive on. Someone will make a sign that reads, "I'm sorry lads, we kept it up as long as we could. Nearest Tesco, fifteen miles east. Buy potatoes from Italy for as little as 15 cents."

Many a Sunday, Granddad got up from the table, answering the hall door halfway through his dinner for someone who'd run out of milk, or tea, or both. He was a breed of gentleman that attended every funeral from Carraroe to Cork. He refused no one. My mother was always saying what fine people had gone before us; what a shame to her I must have been.

I had my eyes closed, listening to the hum of the soft-drinks fridge when the door was given a rap. One of the Varleys was standing there, still in his wellingtons, with his bike left outside and a look of shame brought in with him.

"I'm sorry lad, I was headed for the shop over the road, knowing where ye'd be."

Varley shook my hand, taking in my black suit with a tactful amount of surprise.

"No finer man in the parish than your grandfather."

"You're alright sure," I said, "you were good to come to the house."

Only looking back do you realise how glad you are people come to wakes. They take a bit of the grief with them, shaking it out of your palms and into theirs, carried off to their own homes and corners.

I let him pick up a loaf, two litres of milk and a packet of Benson. It turns out Varley and Granddad were in the same class in school. Varley leaned against the door, his goods in a white plastic bag, telling me stories: when Granddad invited all his neighbours to watch the All-Ireland on the first TV set around, when he spared a family from feeling hunger, when he'd had half the parish on his books living on tick and never a word said, when he'd wait until they sold their calves in spring to pay him back. I knew where some dusty ledgers were kept to prove it.

"Your grandfather had the first ice cream fridge in the whole of Connaught, you know. They came from all over that summer, the excitement of it."

I saw my own summers when he said it, Granddad standing over the kitchen table, cutting the block of vanilla and pressing it into a sandwich of wafers; the ice cream leaking along his fingers.

"Do you mind?" I asked as Varley unwrapped the fags. We lit up inside.

"I'm sure your mother's glad to have you home," he said, just as the hearse rounded the corner. I'd switched the lights off, a due show of respect paid to all the dead who passed on their way in that black chariot, watching as his body passed us one last time and through the climbing smoke I saluted it. My mother, I knew, would be too furious to glance our way. Is my plot to be beside him, I thought, watching the cortege wind over the bridge, are those who share blood obliged to share earth and clay as well? We're awful at that in this country, letting go. We think continuity satisfies the ghosts like libations.

"You'll do him proud," Varley said before he left, "when you take over the shop someday."

I clamped the filter between molars and the taste of tar ran into my saliva. I felt it harden in my throat and spread throughout me, like filling a pothole. Surely, Varley saw. No, I suppose guilt and grief look about the same on me today. In the church they said, "Sure, you'll say a few words." I had nothing prepared. I just got up to the microphone and repeated the words I'd heard Granddad use, quoting Donleavy: "Ireland is a place where the dead are forever living."

"Running low on carrots, old man," I whispered, walking the length of the shop. The walls needed painting, new units installed, and half of the lights were blown. I stopped to scratch a stray sticker off a shelf, watching the stubborn glue give way. Maybe I could have run it, I thought, in a time when Lidl and Aldi receipts weren't bursting wallets. Back when people chucked out the punts from their pockets, fingers sorting the turf dust from the silver. You saw a lot of hands handling money. The old stock, their fingernails were like slabs of exposed rock on the hills around this place, worn by the elements to reveal what lies beneath. Now you saw shellacs pinching cards and asking for cash back.

There was a graveyard in the stockroom. Granddad never seemed to mind too much. He seemed to understand that black flies were coming to curl their backs there for as long as he could remember. Store-room knowledge that had now fallen to me. I grabbed a strip of muslin cloth from the kitchen, orange peel dried into it from the mother's annual marmalade making. She'd only just started dissolving the sugar and peels on the stove when it happened. I was in the hospital with him and, through the phone, heard the shatter of the Pyrex jug she let drop. The muslin effused the tangy citron incense as I climbed the ladder. There they were, scattered like a bag of raisins on the windowsill between the crisps and toilet rolls. Black specks, legs raised, wings blown to the dusty floor, the sun high enough to deprive them of shadows.

When I was younger, much younger, I climbed the sides of this valley and at each summit wished with closed eyes, just before the lip, that some great sight would lie beyond it. Forests, craters, and canyons with carriage-trains steaming off in the distance; dark figures on horseback preparing to raid it. Now I am older, much older, and know you hold dreams like a surgeon holds hearts, working in the dark, snipping threads that hold them down, and hoping you don't hit the arteries of your loved ones. I hadn't told them. I'd lied.

"No, Mam, the ticket was one-way. Sure, I'll stay for a bit. I'll stay."

I set off up the valley towards the mountains with the muslin parcel in hand, my eyes trained on their heathered brows, looking for answers from those that have seen all this before. And I wondered at those valley-men, pushing at the boundaries of their universe by labour of back and hand, charging their stonewalls up those vertical faces.

*Helen Hughes*
*Galway*

*Home*

## Nomad

*Is this the kitchen?*
he says.
I thought he was joking.
Big man of my childhood,
my gentle father.

*I have difficulty with orientation,*
he says.
Astray in the house
he has lived in
for thirty-seven years.

*Where will I put my things?*
with laden arms,
he asks
his wife
of fifty-two years.

*He's okay,*
she says.
*It's just his short term memory;*
*he's still himself.*
I wish.

*Aideen Henry*
*Claddagh, Co. Galway*

## New Tricks for Me and Ma

*Nerina Burke*
*Galway*

# Home

The following three poems are inspired by the Irish legend of Midir, son of the Dagda Mór, and his two wives, Étain and Fúamnach. The poems concentrate on the part of the legend where Midir brings Étain home and she meets his first wife, Fúamnach. Consumed with jealousy, Fúamnach conspires against her beautiful rival. She turns her into a pool of water and when it evaporates, Étain emerges as an exquisite purple butterfly.

---

## Étain Moves in with Fúamnach

If I can feel at home here
all will be well, all calm.
Fúamnach guides me to a chair,
"Sit down at my house's heart."

Beautiful in a grey way,
she freezes me to the bone.
Midir is mistaken, I'm sure he is.
"She won't mind, she'll welcome you.

She knows tradition and custom."
This chair is in the centre,
well placed among all circles.
Maybe I'll move it a little.

*No*, she seems to shriek but
her voice is low, measured,
the noise is in her eyes only.
Her rebuff cuts me.

I had better sit in this chair,
seems to be her wish, a small
matter to make Madame happy.
I lower myself onto the seat,

a smile suffuses her face, soft,
pale, like a bowl of cream
left out for Samhain's mysteries.

She pats his arm, looks right

into my heart, seems to purr,
"The seat of a good woman
hast thou come into, Étain."
Her declaration of herself.

I'll sit awhile, let her know.

## Étain in Fúamnach's Thrall

I feel so funny, so strange,
I'm seated in the room's centre.
Nothing moves, she grins as if
all happiness has befallen her.

Her eyes, they are so dangerous,
like a cat about to tease a mouse,
wearied by a hundred escapes.
I'm no mouse, I'll stand up,

thank her for her best chair,
make my excuses, move to the door.
But I cannot move, all about me
is whirling like worlds gone away.

She leaves, sees Midir off.
"She's well looked after,"
she says, touches his elbow.
She looks back at me.

Her eyes are my drowning place.
I think to call out to him,
"Wait, wait I'll leave with you."
No sound from my trapped voice.

*Home*

He's gone, she's gone. I'm here,
caught in the centre of circles,
will not stop their whirling.
I feel I'm at the bottom of a lake,

pegged down by a thousand stones.
All as one, holding me forever.

~

## Étain in Fúamnach's Spell

The circles have stopped whirring.
I'm steady, I'll hold the armrest
and leave this chair, never again
seat myself in its nightmare.

But what is happening to me?
My voice drains from me,
flows to one long scream,
silent in its vehemence.

I clasp my hands, they won't bend,
they fall in strange ways,
they flow from my arms,
my wrists, my elbows, melting.

I'll stand up, race from
terrors in Fúamnach's house.
My feet won't carry me.
My legs are streams.

What am I looking upon?
My heart flows from me.
I can't clasp this chair's edges,
can't hoist myself into the air.

I seem to be all sea, perhaps

I'm in a black faint, stretched
out on the floor, yes, that's it.
I'm not in the real world.

I'll look but my eyes won't open,
they're like closed water lilies on
a sleeping lake, motionless.
What has come upon me?

Why have my limbs weakened,
nearly weak as water?
I can't stand up or look about.
I can't move, am I paralysed?

What can be happening to me?
This chair has brought ill on me.
I can't walk from this room,
wetness overwhelms me.

*Ann Egan*
*Kildare*

*Home*

## La Belle Bitch

With no time to double back, I cut a clear path.
Easy to track. Exhaustion bends my mind to see
shadows flit between the broken lines of trees.
I feel her, feel her lurk in winter's rare amber.

She came to me last night. There were mere inches
between us. She seemed almost gentle as she froze
my breath. "One word," she said, and plucked a purse
from her mouth. It was soft and brown as a mouse.

She pressed it to my cheek. I was too tired, too tired
to flinch. Her arm was blue and barbed with scars.
That was the first time I slept. Now I search in circles
keeping my distance from her crackling presence.

*Niamh Boyce*
*Athy*

# Housey

*Nerina Burke*
*Galway*

*Home*

## Sunroom, Midnight

Here in the house of my youth
the echo of rain hisses like a mad ghost,
sick for the past.

Candle flame flickers,
silent, miniature.
Collie lies
eyes open by my feet.

The morning came bright with
red cedar, blackjack oak, and the awakening
of a mountain laurel chaparral.

Ten thousand yawning blossoms stretched down
to laughter on the lake as an old man yelled
about a fish fixed to the end of his grandson's line.

Honeysuckle and morning glory swayed
open-mouthed over footbridge logs and cedar boughs,
and sunfish watched as stones like shooting stars
skipped above and vanished forever.

Tonight, the violet smear of the Milky Way,
the specter of slow-churning eternity in the skylight,
is gone.

Midnight smacks on every glass pane –
black rectangles until a flash punctures the room
and the pale ceiling shivers.

After the slow unfurl of a short memory,
thunder pangs.

My old dog went deaf in this room.

A lightning bolt took his ears, split

an oak in half a few feet
and years from where I now sit.

Only days later,
the shaggy dog of my youth
heard no rustle when he fell like rain.

*David J. Doyle*
*New Jersey Pine Barrens*

*Home*

## Little Maverick Hen

Little maverick hen
*undersized but valiant*
scorns the hens
*overfed and unintelligent.*
She nests with the ducks,
gobbles their food,
unfazed by their filthy water.

These shortening winter days
she pecks purposefully,
an explorer searching out
her own terrain in the shrubs.
At night, as the hens
file into their coop
she refuses to surrender
to the call to roost,
placing herself in the path
of unknown nocturnal terrors.

She waits for me each morning,
hopping impatiently,
every speckled feather
on her crested neck
unruffled.

*Faye Boland*
*Kenmare, Co. Kerry*

## I Used to Sit by the Water and Watch the Waves Rolling By

When I was younger I used to walk out to the lake
When nobody would notice I was gone.
I'd look out across the water to faraway shores
And breathe in the air like each breath was my last.

It was always the most beautiful place I'd ever known,
A place I loved to be alone;
That beauty would calm me in my darkest days.

I used to dream of drowning in those waters,
When the voices in my head would get so loud
That their screaming twisted and distorted every thought in my head
To the point that I didn't know who I was anymore.
I still don't.

I stopped going there a few years ago,
Though I'm not sure why.
Maybe I just didn't have the time.

I remember walking under street-lights in the heart of last winter,
When I came to the water's edge.
I stayed until dawn before making my way back
To the place that I called home,
A cold bed in a mould-riddled room
That made it hard to breathe,
A window that let in no light so it was always dark,
Even in the day.

I still dream about the water,
When the anxiety sets in.
I find myself at home there,
Though I never learnt to swim.

*Vincent Hughes*
*Mayo*

*Home*

# Dringeen Bay

*Vincent Hughes*
*Mayo*

*Home*

## Seeking Light

Sleet swoops
across a bleached sky,
my cherry blossom rusty
with rain.

I seek colour
in rosy sunsets
and in juice squeezed
from blood oranges.
I shine fireside mirrors,
buff wooden floors
sparkle glass tabletops
polish chestnut sofas
and settle in the sheen
of my sitting room.

I burn a jasmine scented candle,
kindle flames in the wood stove,
place a patchwork blanket
around my knees,
in lush green fields
of budding springtime.
I see sand and blue seas
in a collection of shells
piled high in my crystal bowl.
Cobalt skies flash
from pots of grape hyacinths
and the yellow glow of warmth
nods from tête-à-tête on the windowsill.

On stormy days,
I seek the light within.

*Máire Morrissey-Cummins*
*Greystones, Co. Wicklow*

## Nature's Healing Hands

Lost and alone
morning rises,
I force myself outdoors
to dispel my angst.

I trudge beneath November skies,
flat, grey, devoid of light,
the constant threat of rain.

My feet shift to a steady pace
down long, leafy roads
draped in autumn,
Leaves ablaze.
I shelter among rows of copper, gold
and crispy reds.
I stroll sunlit paths of fallen sycamore,
thickets shimmer scarlet with hips and haws,
leaves whisper and sing
spin all around me
and I am caressed,
by nature's abundance.
My hand strokes a moss-covered wall
drenched in dew,
I breathe in the earthy scent
no longer forlorn,

and up above, a trickle of light
curls on a lip of cloud,
fields shine silver,
coated in drizzle.

I return to an empty house,
my heart tingles

*Home*

with the changing season,

I vow to bend with the wind.

*Máire Morrissey-Cummins*
*Greystones, Co. Wicklow*

ROPES
2014
Home

Thank You for Your Donations!

ROPES would like to thank all of the businesses who helped support the journal through advertising and other non-monetary means.
Your generosity is kindly appreciated.

# Contributors

## Faye Boland

Faye Boland has had poems published in THE SHOp, Revival, Crannóg and Orbis. She was shortlisted in 2013 for the Poetry on the Lake XIII International Poetry Competition. She is a member of Clann na Farraige writers group in Kenmare, County Kerry. In 2007, she left a university career to become a homemaker. She wears many hats: cook, cleaner, nurse, educator, gardener and carer of animals and fowl. Her experiences at home and the landscape there inspire her poems.

## Niamh Boyce

Niamh writes poetry, stories, plays and novels. She was awarded the Hennessy XO New Irish Writer of the Year in 2012 for her poetry, and her debut novel The Herbalist won Best Newcomer of 2013 at the Irish Book Awards.

## Dean Buckley

Dean Buckley is a writer of fiction and poetry, originally from Cahir, County Tipperary and currently living in Galway City, where he studies creative writing at NUI Galway. Once, when Dean was trying to walk up some stairs, his body disagreed and threw him very hard into the adjacent wall. Some say you can still hear his plaintive cries echoing when the boreal winds billow in the chimney stacks: "Bollocks, bollocks, bollocks..." His other interests include browser games and competitive debating.

## Nerina Burke

Nerina Burke is an East Londoner by birth who has made Galway her home for most of her life. She believes that for her, home is the place that consistently holds the most relevance to one's life. Her images depict relationships to the idea of "home" in a transitional state. A former ROPES contributor, she lives in Moycullen, County Galway.

## Alvy Carragher

Alvy ricochets between writing poetry and weeping over the financial hopelessness of it all. Her poetry has often been put on lists (often long and sometimes short) to assure her that it's of okay quality. She's been published here, there and everywhere (there's a poem in Mexico somewhere). In a fit of self-delusion she ended up on stage and became Connaught's Slam Poetry Champion. Her blog "With all the finesse of a Badger," is allegedly the funniest in the land (according to the Irish Blog Awards) and should provide you with an appreciation for how together your life is.

## Marion Clarke

Warrenpoint artist and writer, Marion Clarke left home in the 1980s to study art in Belfast, but placed her painting on hold to complete a postgraduate diploma in French and business. This led to a job with the Channel Tunnel Contractors in Surrey. She returned home with her family in 2000 and took up painting again. Working mainly in oils and pastel, her location near the Mountains of Mournes inspires both her art and writing.

## Rebecca Connell

Rebecca Connell, 22, is an artist from County Westmeath. She is a student of GMIT and is currently pursuing an honours degree in textile design. She specialises in printed textiles and hopes to attain a career in this area after college. She considers Galway to be her home. She can be contacted at: rebeccaconnell474@gmail.com.

## Trevor Conway

Trevor Conway, a Sligoman living in Galway since 2005, writes mainly poetry, fiction and songs. Subjects he is drawn to include nature, creativity, football and people/society, especially the odd ways in which we look at the world. His work has appeared in magazines and anthologies across Ireland, Austria, India, the UK, the US, and Mexico – where his poems have been translated into Spanish. He has an MA in Writing from NUI Galway. He is a contributing editor for *The Galway Review*, and his first collection of poems is forthcoming from Salmon Poetry.

## Sarah Devaney

Sarah Devaney is a third year student studying undenominated Science in NUI Galway. Her hometown is Castlebar, County Mayo, and she has four siblings who keep home very noisy. For the last few years, since starting college, she has been involved in NUI Galway's Art Society and is currently vice-auditor. Art and drawing are things that she enjoys spending time doing and she hopes to keep it as part of her life in future.

## Declan Devlin

Declan Devlin is a freelance photographer from Letterkenny, County Donegal. Influenced by the surrounding mountains and coastlines, Declan tries to capture natural beauty in his photographs. His work ranges from landscapes and surf photography to wedding and portraits.

## David J. Doyle

David J. Doyle is thrilled to be published in *ROPES* again. He's an American poet and someday novelist with a lot of love for Galway. David would like to thank his fellow 2013 NUI Galway Writing MA graduates, the Black Fort Writers, for their unending inspiration and all the good times.

## Tim Dwyer

Tim Dwyer's recent and upcoming publications include *Crannóg, The Galway Review, Cork Literary Review, Skylight 47, The Linnet's Wings,* The *Stony Thursday Book, Southword* and *Burning Bush 2*. His work-in-progress is *Messages From The Irish Diaspora*. He is a member of Irish American Writers and Artists. He is a psychologist at a correctional facility, grew up in Brooklyn and lives in the Hudson Valley of New York State. His mother was from Gort and his father was from near Loughrea. He will be featured at the March 2015 Over The Edge Reading.

## Ann Egan

Ann Egan, a multi-award winning poet, has held many residencies in counties, hospitals, schools, secure residencies and prisons. Her books are: *Landing the Sea* (Bradshaw Books), *The Wren Women* (Black Mountain Press), *Brigit of Kildare* (Kildare Library and Arts Services) and her latest is 2012's *Telling Time* (Bradshaw Books). She has edited more than twenty books including, *The Midlands Arts and Culture Review* in 2010. She lives in County Kildare.

## Kate Ennals

Kate completed the MA in Writing in NUI Galway last year. She currently facilitates both poetry and writing workshops in her hometown of Cavan (by way of Dublin and London). She has been published in *Crannóg*, *Skylight 47*, *Burning Bush 2* and *The Galway Review*. Kate also is featured in the anthology, *The Adventure Hat*, published by the Black Fort Writers. She is also to be published in the next edition of *Boyne Berries*.

## Maureen Gallagher

Maureen Gallagher's first collection of poetry, *Calling the Tune*, was published by Wordsonthestreet Press in December 2008. Maureen's poetry, literary criticism and short stories have been published in magazines and journals worldwide. She has been shortlisted for and has won many awards for her work, most recently the RTÉ/Penguin Short Story Award (shortlist) and the James Plunkett Award (shortlist). She has tutored creative writing courses in the Galway Education Centre and the Western Writers' Centre.

## Margarita Gokun

A nomad by nature, Margarita Gokun never lives longer than two to four years in any one country. That creates havoc when she packs her canvases but inspiration of a new place almost always makes up for it. Since starting to paint in oil four years ago, Margarita's work has been exhibited at the Museum of Art of Fort Lauderdale (Florida), published in literary and art magazines, and has won contests. Her portfolio can be seen at: http://StoriesAndColors.wordpress.com

*Home*

## Rachael Hanaphy-Pigott

Rachael was born in Dublin and raised in Kilkenny. A professional actor, singer and teacher; her first attempt at poetry, "Bully", was published in 2005. Since then, her work has appeared in publications such as *Rhyme Rag* and the *Kilkenny Poetry Broadsheet*. Home, to the poet, is a mindset: a psychological landscape, persistently altered by time and imminent change, wherein significant associations, memories and loved-ones are enshrined.

## Padhraic Harris

Padhraic Harris practices law in Galway. He wrote short stories and had some published in *Criterion* many years ago while a student at UCG. He then took a break until recently, when he renewed his interest while attending Creative Writing Classes in Galway Technical Institute. He was a featured reader at Over the Edge in September 2013. He has recently been published in *Crannóg 35*.

## Aideen Henry

Aideen Henry's debut collection of poetry, *Hands Moving at the Speed of Falling Snow*, was published by Salmon Poetry in 2010 and that same year she was shortlisted for the Emerging Poetry Section of the Hennessy XO Literary Awards.

## Brian Hickey

Brian Hickey lives in Glasgow, Scotland and was prompted to write "Home for the Night" at Christmas when he saw a number of his city's homeless doing their best to stave off the cold and find enough money for a hot drink, which was in sharp contrast to the well-heeled city shoppers laden down with parcels, making "home" quite different things to those different groups. He writes short stories and non-fiction articles as a panacea for the tedium of frequent business travel.

## Kevin Higgins

Kevin Higgins was born in London in 1967 and lives in Galway, Ireland. He is co-organiser of Over The Edge literary events and teaches poetry workshops at Galway Arts Centre and Creative Writing at Galway Technical Institute. He has published four collections of poems: *The Boy With No Face* (2005), *Time Gentlemen, Please* (2008), *Frightening New Furniture* (2010) and *The Ghost In The Lobby* (2014) all with Salmon Poetry. *Mentioning The War*, a collection of his essays and reviews, was published by Salmon in April 2012. His most recent poetry collection *The Ghost In The Lobby* will be launched by Mick Wallace TD on the final day of Cúirt 2014.

## Helen Hughes

Helen Hughes is a Galway native in her final year of the BA Connect degree in Creative Writing in NUI Galway. She began writing short stories in 2013. This is her first publication. To her, home is a bug you have to write out of your system. If you don't, well, your writing won't get stuck there, but it won't stray very far either.

## Vincent Hughes

Vincent Hughes is a 20-year-old former student of English and Philosophy at NUI Galway. He dropped out of the University last year, after deciding that he wanted to make an attempt to pursue something a little more relevant to his interests. He is currently living in Mayo, where he has spent a lot of the last year writing music and preparing for a course he hopes to get into in September. The rest of his time is divided between movies, writing and (attempted) photography.

## Anne Irwin

Anne Irwin lives in Galway. She studied English and Philosophy in UCG and is a practicing homeopath and teacher. She draws inspiration from nature and everyday life for her poetry, which is often political and sometimes satirical. Her poetry has been published in many magazines. She is a member of the Galway based Tuesday Knights who recently published an anthology of their poetry *Wayword Tuesday*, which was shortlisted for the Writers' Circle Anthology Award, June 2013.

## Anne Marie Kennedy

Anne Marie Kennedy is a student of the MA in Writing at NUI Galway and is thrilled to be published in *ROPES* 2014. She is working on a collection of short stories set between the west of Ireland and America, where she lived for ten years. Her home is a cottage set in a small farm beside the Dunkellin River that she and her husband share with a menagerie of four-legged people.

## Brian Kirk

Brian Kirk is a poet and writer from Dublin. His short fiction has been shortlisted for many awards including the Hennessy New Irish Writer Awards in 2008 and 2011. He was selected for the Poetry Ireland Introductions series in 2013. His novel *Winter Journey* is currently shortlisted for the Today Show/New Island novel competition. His poems and stories have appeared in many journals and anthologies including, *The Sunday Tribune*, *Crannóg*, *The Stony Thursday Book*, *Revival*, *Abridged* (NI), *Southword*, *Boyne Berries*, *Wordlegs*, *Burning Bush 2* and others. He blogs at: http://briankirkwriter.com/.

## Paul Lewis

Paul Lewis was born to loving parents in Cork City and now lives in Galway.

## Aoife McCollum

Aoife McCollum is a recent graduate of NUI Galway; she has completed her degree in English and History. Originally from Donegal, she has been living in Galway for the past four years. She hopes to start her master's degree this September. She would like to work in a publishing or a digital media role in the future. She has also set her sights on travelling for a few years.

## Christopher Meehan

Christopher Meehan currently resides in East Galway but grew up in the seaside town of Kilkee, County Clare. In 2012 he was shortlisted for the Fish International Poetry Prize, and in 2013 he was placed third in the Over The Edge New Writer of the Year competition. His poems have been published in *Skylight 47*, *Boyne Berries*, *Crannóg* and online in *The Galway Review*.

## Máire Morrissey-Cummins

Máire Morrissey-Cummins lives in Greystones, County Wicklow. She has been writing since 2010 and has been published in *A New Ulster*, *The First Cut*, *Wordlegs*, *Everydaypoets*, *Your Daily Poem*, *Bray Arts Journal*, *The Galway Review*, *A Hundred Gourds*, *Lynx* and many other online and print magazines. She loves to get lost in words or paint. She is listed in the top 100 European creative haiku writers for 2012 and 2013. When painting, she loves watercolour and acrylic, and has developed a stained glass style following the flow of the pigment on the page. She is married with two adult children.

## Fiona Nic Dhonnacha

Fiona is from An Cheathrú Rua in Galway, and graduated from the MA in Literature and Publishing last year. Before that she completed a BA in English and Irish. She enjoys reading and writing both in English and as Gaeilge, and always gets inspiration from a walk on the beach or a drive around Connemara. She currently works as a copywriter and freelance editor. Fiona can be contacted at f.nicdhonnacha@gmail.com.

## Jessamine O Connor

Jessamine O Connor left Dublin for rural Sligo in 1999, where she lives with her family in an old train station at Lough Gara. Winner of the iYeats and Francis Ledwidge awards in 2011, she's come close in several other competitions and is published widely. Most recent journals include *Agenda*, *Shot Glass Journal*, *The Galway Review*, *Crannóg* and *The Stony Thursday Book*. She facilitates a weekly creative writing group from home, and her chapbook *Hellsteeth* is available from: www.jessamineoconnor.com.

## Kate Quigley

Kate Quigley is originally from County Meath, Ireland, but currently lives in a forest in Poland for reasons unknown, even to herself. She is a graduate of NUI Galway's BA Connect in Creative Writing, but also dabbles in photography and painting. Her work has previously appeared in publications such as *The Stinging Fly*, *Orbis* and *THE SHOp*.

## Ruth Quinlan

Ruth Quinlan is from Tralee, County Kerry and holds an MA in Writing from NUI Galway. She won the Hennessy First Fiction Literature Award in 2013 and was shortlisted for the 2012 and 2014 Cúirt New Writing Fiction Prize. Her work has been published by the *Irish Independent*, *ROPES*, *Crannóg*, *Skylight 47*, *Emerge Literary Journal*, *Thresholds* and *Scissors and Spackle*. She has also contributed both fiction and poetry to several anthologies.

## Brooke Randel

Brooke Randel is a short story writer and copywriter. She studied advertising and English at Penn State University and has won awards for her copywriting work. She currently lives in Philadelphia.

## Máire T. Robinson

Máire T. Robinson is a graduate of NUI Galway (MA in Writing). She is the author of the short story chapbook, *Your Mixtape Unravels My Heart* (Doire Press, 2013), and the founding editor of *Short Story Ireland*. She lives and works in Dublin City.

## Breda Spaight

Breda Spaight is a poet and novelist from County Limerick. Her poetry has appeared in *The Stony Thursday Book*, *Revival* and *Skylight 47*. Two of her poems are forthcoming in *THE SHOp* (2014). She was shortlisted in the Listowel Single Poem Competition.

# Jerry Wemple

Jerry Wemple is the author of three poetry collections, most recently *The Artemas Poems* (Finishing Line Press, 2014). His poems and creative nonfiction appear in numerous journals and anthologies. Although he has travelled to thirteen countries and lived in several regions of the United States, Wemple now resides in his native Susquehanna River Valley, where he teaches creative writing at Bloomsburg University of Pennsylvania. For more of his work, visit his website: www.jwemple.com.

# The ROPES Team

## Project Manager

Siobhán Keenan

## Editorial

Sarah Brady
Alison Buck
Shauna Daly
Shauna Kenneally
Damien Lynam
Lauren Mateer

## Advertising, Sales and Marketing

Niamh Callaghan
Nuala Cronin
Ciara O Riordan

## Design

Rachel Dillon
Moira Morley

## Production

Sarah Brady

# ROPES 2014

Proceeds from the sale of this literary journal will go to COPE Galway.